Chasing Glenn Beck

*A Personal Experiment in Reclaiming
Our Hijacked Political Conversation*

ෆ ౸

Michael Charney

Riddle Brook Publishing
Bedford, NH

Publishers Cataloging-in-Publication Data

Charney, Michael, 1958-
    Chasing Glenn Beck : a personal experiment in
reclaiming our hijacked political conversation/Michael
Charney. – 1st trade pbk. Ed.
    p. cm.
    LCCN 2011960116
    ISBN-13: 978-0-9847927-0-2
    ISBN-10: 0-9847927-0-8

    1. Communication in politics--United States- Humor.
2. Social media--United States--Humor. 3. Beck, Glenn--
Humor. I. Title

JA85.2.U6C43.2012   320.973'014
                        QBI11-600219

Library of Congress Catalog Number: 2011960116
ISBN-13: 978-0-9847927-0-2 (Trade Paper)
ISBN-13: 978-0-9847927-1-9 (eBook)

Riddle Brook Publishing LLC, Bedford NH

www.riddlebrookpublishing.com

www.chasingglennbeck.com

For Gabe and Chris

"*We cannot question falsity when facts are our beliefs and our beliefs are facts.*"

--Mary Ann Reilly

"*I could give a flying crap about the political process...We're an entertainment company.*"

--Glenn Beck

CONTENTS

AUTHOR'S NOTE

hasing Glenn Beck recounts my three-month experience discussing politics with hundreds of other people on Twitter,
and contains a number of tweets, quotes, and excerpts from
various websites. I have changed all of the names (including Twitter
"@names") except in cases where the individual is a public figure or
is someone from my own past whom I think might get a kick out of
seeing his or her name in print. However, there are millions and
millions of Twitter users (and more every day), so while I've tried to
ensure that none of the invented names actually belong to a real
person, I can't be completely sure. If it turns out that I've attributed
something to someone accidentally, I'm sorry. I didn't mean to.

The tweets themselves have undergone some modification in
order to make them more readable, though the changes never affect
either tone or content. I've spelled out most abbreviations (Do you
really need to read the word "gr8" one more time?), cleaned up a bit
of the grammar, and inserted a word here and there when I thought
clarity demanded it. I've also deleted most of the links that people
commonly insert into their tweets. (No offense to owl.ly and bit.ly,
but your crap is impossible to read and totally screws up any
narrative flow.) As a result of these changes, some tweets end up

breaking through the 140-character barrier. I figured that was better than abject confusion.

As far as the facts in the book—well, facts are a funny thing. Writing in real time creates an interesting paradox when coupled with the iterations that a book goes through during its various editing cycles. When editing, an author has the advantage (and risk) of hindsight and must be careful not to let later events affect the thoughts and emotions that emerged in the moment. I've tried to be as honest with myself as possible, maintaining the thread and flow of reality as it happened. While I have occasionally moved some of the discourse from one chapter to another (but never by more than one week), I have kept all of the calendar events exactly when they occurred. My memory both benefits and suffers from the passing of time. I expect I've made some mistakes, but if I have, I've done so honestly. As you'll discover, memory is a funny thing: the more you remember something, the truer it becomes...

And, finally, the opinions in the book are my own. I have no special standing, no special expertise. I just have something to say, and feel like saying it.

INTRODUCTION:
MARCH 15, 2011

I'm not a nice person. I know this because Glenn Beck told me so.

Okay, perhaps he didn't tell me directly. What actually happened was this: in early March our resident emperor-pundit (and self-described rodeo clown) suggested that if we hadn't gone and screwed up the whole following-the-Commandments thing, then perhaps our angry and vengeful God wouldn't have slaughtered the innocents in Japan, where a recent tsunami had devastated large stretches of seacoast.

Yep. You heard right. Beck was suggesting that God passes His verdicts on the world in the form of earthquakes and tidal waves.

"Hey, you know that stuff we're doing?" Beck asked his listeners. "Not really working out real well." He then went on to add that "What God does is God's business. But I'll tell you this...there's a message being sent."

I know he's not the first to render such opinions; people like Jerry Falwell, Jimmy Swaggart, and Pat Robertson have all said similar things in the past. Falwell, for example, informed his faithful that "AIDS is the wrath of a just God against homosexuals," and Pat Robertson once drooled that the floods in New Orleans were "a sign that God is tired of seeing his creation mocked by the Mardi Gras and its perverted display of debauchery and exposed breasts." If statements like Beck's aren't that unusual, why then should he, in particular, piss me off so much?

It's because Glenn Beck is an entertainer. While the others said things that were abhorrent and stupid, they were at least speaking within the sincerity of their own beliefs. But Beck isn't. He's shtick. He's pomp. He said as much back in the April 26, 2010 issue of *Forbes* magazine. "I could give a flying crap about the political process," he told the reporter. "We're an entertainment company."

When I think of Glenn Beck, I get an image of Uriah Heep but with Bozo's big red clown nose. Imagine it: Dickensian sleaze with an overpowering aura of farce. On the one hand, Beck claims to be "just so 'umble," while at the same time you can sense the devious machinery clicking away behind those eyes. It's hard to look away, mostly because you never know what he's going to do next. No wonder people are so interested in him. In many ways it's an undeniably fascinating combination: innocence, self-deprecation, and cunning in equal parts, all standing before a microphone and broadcasting to millions while alternating smiles and tears on cue. It's all just too perfect.

That got me thinking. It has to be an act, a persona. He couldn't be that extreme, that far to the right. He has to be something else. And if it *is* just a persona, just an act, could I undo, even a little bit, what Beck has wrought? Could I make anyone believe that Glenn Beck was not what he seemed to be?

So today I've decided to take a stab at the emperor.

March 15: The Ides of March, a day marked in history by the murder of Julius Caesar, stabbed to death in the Theater of Pompeii by Brutus, Longinus, and as many as sixty others. Julius, it turns out, was not a nice guy, and a number of people decided he should be taken down a peg or two. So they did.

When the Romans decided they'd had enough of their self-proclaimed emperor and his outsized ego, they put together a movement to try to change things. They used the social network of the time (I think they called it "talking" back then), and with a bit of carefully wrought conspiracy rid themselves of a Caesar. I'm curious to see if we can do that again, even if only in the smallest way. Beck has gotten my goat by suggesting that God is killing thousands upon thousands of innocents just because we go to the mall on Sunday or occasionally look with envy at our neighbor's new Lexus, and I feel like reacting.

So I'm starting a little experiment today, just to see what happens. I'm going to use Twitter—today's version of the Roman forum—to see if I can create a groundswell of belief in the idea that Glenn Beck isn't as he appears, that maybe he's just an actor playing to the crowd, hoping for applause while cashing the checks.

I've established both a Gmail account: BeckIsALib@Gmail.com, and a Twitter account: @BeckIsALib. I'm not trying to do this surreptitiously and I'm not trying to pretend I'm somebody I'm not. I just want to see if a trickle of carefully selected information—along with a bit of hyperbole—can shift the wind: Glenn Beck is a liberal. Glenn Beck believes in global warming. Glenn Beck cares about animals and the environment. Glenn Beck is an actor playing a part.

I've chosen to use Twitter because there is no platform in the world with the same potential for rapid and widespread communication. The ability to find and connect with thousands and thousands of like-minded people in a matter of hours is unprecedented in our history. If an idea is to go viral, Twitter is the way to do it. It's the closest thing we have to a social networking speed of light.

To kick things off I sent a single tweet. It said, simply:

BeckIsALib: 1st Tweet- #GlennBeck. For any who follow, this is an experiment. This is today's only tweet. More tweets on Beck begin tomorrow.

The only thing special about the tweet is the use of the "#," or "hash tag," a Twitter marker that others can use to quickly identify tweets on a particular topic.

That's it. Simple, honest, short, and sweet.

I've set myself a few rules. First, I don't plan to tell anyone I'm doing this (other than my wife), but, if asked, I'll confirm that it's me playing this little game. Second, I will not "follow" anyone on Twitter except for Glenn Beck himself. Since there's a common Twitterquette that suggests mutual following, I don't want anyone to feel they have to follow me just because I've followed them. I want the idea to carry the day. Third, I will not invent any quotes and attribute them to Beck. That would be wrong. I'll probably twist a few of his quotes to suit my purpose, but if I didn't, then how would I have any fun?

Tomorrow I'll check back and report on what, if anything, has happened. Will I have a follower or two? Will people wonder who I am and what I'm doing? Will I get hate mail? Even worse, will I merely be ignored?

I'm going to let this run for three months, until the Ides of June. Three months: that seems about right.

WEEK ONE:
TAKING A STAB @ IT

I'm no longer alone. I've just checked Twitter and my follower count has ticked to "1."

@KimRavenscroft appears to be quite the Glenn Beck fan. I feel a surge of both delight and relief as I check her recent tweets, but both quickly fade when I realize that her last post was six days ago, so I have to assume that she doesn't actually know she's following me yet. Most likely she has a rule set up to automatically "follow" anyone with the "#GlennBeck" tag in their post.

I didn't even know you could set up an automatic "follow" until a couple of days ago, and that's only one of several interesting Twitter capabilities I've recently discovered. It turns out that Twitter is far richer than I thought. I've been using it for a while as a way of supporting my wife's consulting business but had never really taken the time to explore it fully. I knew the basics but not much more, and saw Twitter more as a requirement than an interest.

I've always been this way with technology. I still have a basic cell phone because I just want to make phone calls. I don't care about texting or paging or uploading mobile photos of a blurry sunset, nor do I want to LOL with people while I'm driving or sitting in a movie theater. I have an iPad because I received it as a gift, but I'm still not sure what the big deal is; it seems rather like the phone I don't want, only with a nasty thyroid condition. I was also the last person I know to get a DVR, a high-quality digital camera, or a wireless network for my home.

All of this is ironic considering I've spent my entire career in high tech, yet that, too, was an accident. When I started out as a recruiter back in the eighties, it just so happened that they needed someone to recruit computer programmers, so that's where I ended up. It was interesting enough so I learned what I needed to and stayed with it.

These days I use Twitter to refer people to our blog or our website in order to create a bit of branding presence or sometimes to identify marketing opportunities. I do understand its power; I just don't really know how to exercise that power very well.

For this experiment I'd need to learn.

Twitter is the world communicating 140 characters at a time, a unique concept with an underlying paradox. Communication should be deep and thoughtful, the opposite of what you expect to see when truncated into a series of snippets. And yet amazing things happen in the Twittersphere. Entire nations have felt the weight—and sometimes the sting—of these all-too-brief tweets. As early as 2007 *PC Magazine* said that "this small idea has blossomed into a hugely popular phenomenon, with its users covering the entire Earth."

Despite Twitter's sometimes world-shaping influence, most of us don't really have that many interesting things to say. Nevertheless, *homo eavesdropperus* can't seem to get enough. Twitter is communication by Gummi Bear: you know they don't taste that good, but you keep chowing down on them anyway, one after another, hoping for a sudden burst of flavor that rarely comes.

To get started on Twitter you first have to become an "at," which you do by creating an account and choosing a name. To this name Twitter adds a character: the @ sign. Twitter's @ puts the "social" in "social network;" it's how you communicate with others in the

Twittersphere. Having an @name isn't enough, though. There are two other critical parts to your Twitter persona. The first is the icon that appears next to a person's tweets. Twitter gives you a default icon but it's just an ugly little white egg with any one of several pastel colored backgrounds, a billboard that essentially says, "I don't know what I'm doing, I'm rarely logged in, and I don't know what all the fuss is about but my cousin Richie insisted that I have a Twitter account." It's the Twitter equivalent of invisibility. One needs a personal icon, something representative and noticeable. Many people use their own faces or a family photo, often with pets or grinning children held in loving embrace. Others choose aggressive avatars, some looking like they've just leapt from the pages of Frank Miller's *Sin City*. Companies use logos. In the pool I was wading through there were a large number of American flags, eagles, battleships, and "Don't Tread on Me" signs, along with a few too many bastardized images of Barack Obama.

I needed a politically neutral icon, one that would render me visible (as the egg would not) but still not offend anyone. So I settled on a graphic of the word "Respect" printed boldly in cursive, black letters on a white background.

Completing a persona requires constructing your bio, a brief statement about who you are and what you're about that appears on your profile and helps identify you to others. Bios across the Twitterverse contain just about anything you can imagine and can be playful ("This week I feel like being a Socialist, Communist, Marxist, Liberal. Always way far Left of the Right Wing"), informative ("College student interested in technology, politics, and journalism. Social Media Director and much more."), or just plain rude ("Liberal living in Georgia. Calling out a$$holes. Bashing Christian sheeple.") After weighing several options, I chose something akin to a vision statement:

BeckIsALib: Preserving conservatism by exposing the hypocrisy of the conservative media.

The underlying idea is both simple and important: lies, distortions, and hypocrisy from the far right hurt the conservative cause. They turn the party's right wing into right wingnuts and contribute to the stereotype that all conservatives are, as Barack Obama infamously said during the 2008 campaign, bitter people clinging to their guns and religion. I'm also hoping that my Twitter biography raises curiosities; a chance to explain myself means that I'm engaging, and engaging means that I'm heard.

With an account up and running and a well-chosen icon and bio in place, I'm now officially a tweep[1] and can start tweeting. People tweet for numerous reasons: some are interested in selling something, others in creating a brand or image for their service, still others, like me, are marketing ideas. However, the vast majority of tweets that I see are about people connecting merely for the sake of connecting. Danny just finished a killer spinach salad at the Cheesecake Factory and wants everyone to know. Rita just cannot believe that Kirstie Alley didn't walk away with the trophy on *Dancing with the Stars*. Stuff like that. It makes it somewhat difficult to rise above the noise at times, which is why getting "followed" is so important.

The big thing on Twitter is the follow. People obsess about their follower count the way NASCAR fans obsess about pit crews. When someone follows you, it means that he or she will see your tweets appear in a vertical scrolling list—what Twitter calls the "timeline." Beth Pulsifer of Red Moon Antiques covers it quite nicely in a blog posting from August of 2009:

---

[1] A portmanteau word constructed from "tweet" and "peeps" (or "people"). Originally the term was a pejorative but is now generally accepted as referring to anyone actively using Twitter. Like many Twitterisms the word is overly cute, though not as gag-worthy as "twaffic" or "tweetheart."

Following is truly an art. Those who are serious about using Twitter to promote their business quickly learn that numbers mean everything. The more followers you have, the more exposure you'll receive. And it's not only direct exposure to individual followers – what also helps you as a business person is the indirect exposure you receive when a follower re-tweets you to "their" followers.

The easiest way to get followers, it turns out, is to follow others yourself. I know it sounds simplistic, but it's true. If you search for others with common interests then you can follow them. They will see that you've done so and, in many cases, will follow you back. It's not required, but mutual follows are pretty common, a genial part of Twitterquette. You can quickly build a follower list this way.

Unfortunately, my self-imposed rule prevents me from using this technique. Still, I'm curious to see who's out there, and I'm also looking for savvy hash tags to insert into my tweets, and for that I need to search the Twitterverse.

Searching in Twitter is both simple and tricky, rather like the game of Go. Learning the basic moves is a breeze but mastering the intricacies is much more difficult. First of all, Twitter can only search through about a week's worth of tweets. There are just too many out there to handle more than that, so if you're looking for anything older you won't have much luck. And given that Twitter is so damned big, you can never know how much of it you're really seeing—or not seeing.

The system does provide a good start, though: the hash tag. In Twitter, the hash sign (#) is used for internal Twitter searches, and you can set up and save a search for a particular tag, essentially allowing you to monitor the tag as if you had subscribed to it. So if anyone wants to see everything that mentions Glenn Beck (at least in the past week), they can search for, or subscribe to, the tag "#GlennBeck." That's why I'm putting that tag into all of my tweets. It's how I expect to be found.

The other thing about Twitter is that it has spawned an entire ecosystem of applets and add-ons, all designed to enrich the Twitter experience. There's Tweetdeck and Hootsuite and TwitterCounter. There's Twitterholic and Twello and TwitterFox. Many of these satellite programs let you manage how you use Twitter, and will even do some things for you automatically, such as auto-respond with a robust "Thanks!" whenever someone follows you. There are also programs that keep track of the Twitterverse so you don't have to, checking to see if anyone has used a particular hash tag, and, if so, to automatically set up a follow. My guess is that this is what happened with @KimRavenscroft. Now the questions will be, first, will she "unfollow" me once she's sees what I'm about and, second, if she keeps the follow, will she find any of my entries tantalizing enough to "RT" me?

"RT" is the last of the big-time actions on Twitter, and arguably the most powerful if your goal is influence building. "RT" stands for "retweet," and it's the equivalent of forwarding an email to your entire contacts list. The goal, deep down, of every tweeter (I don't care what you say) is to write something so clever, so pithy, so perfectly suited for 140 characters that someone (or multiple someones) on your follower list will retweet it to all of their followers, and then, perhaps, some of those people to their followers.

Then the Twitterverse may actually know that you exist.

If my experiment is to work, then I'll certainly need my tweets retweeted—and often. But first I need some followers of my own, tweeps who can experience my brilliant wit first-hand. Yesterday's tweet resulted in a single follower; hopefully today's will generate more. I've sent two.[2] The first was this:

BeckIsALib: #GlennBeck is an entertainer—and a good one. How can we separate person from persona?

That's it. Unassuming and unpretentious, it starts to set up my premise by defining Beck as an entertainer.

I followed with this:

BeckIsALib: "We're an entertainment company," said #GlennBeck. Does he really mean this? Does he even believe the things he says?

C8 &O

The next morning breaks with the sound of a delivery truck rumbling down our dirt road. It's early, but I get up anyway. It's all I can do not to jump online pre-coffee, but I'm just not that witty with the sun barely risen. I've tried. Seriously. Nothing happens. I'm so incoherent at this hour that my wife has wisely decided not to engage me in any conversation that requires a decision more involved than "Do you think we should call the dogs in? They're barking at the neighbor kids again." I trudge downstairs instead, flip on the coffee, and wait for the brew cycle to finish. Once poured, the coffee and I settle in to read for a bit, then watch the news for half an hour or so. The morning begins to slip away.

---

[2] I'm aware that dropping two tweets and expecting anything to happen is a bit like standing on New Jersey's Long Beach Island, dropping a penny into the water and then expecting that a Maori in New Zealand will pick it up the next day. Still, it's a start.

Shortly before lunch I log on to my Twitter account. Not much has happened overnight; I still have the one follower but no other activity. I can only assume that @Kim still doesn't have a clue that her automated program has tapped my #GlennBeck tag. I dread the thought of seeing my follower count drop back to zero once she finds out.

It's time to launch a couple of new tweets into the Twittersphere in the hopes that they'll land on a few not-so-deaf ears. I'm going to add a new hash tag as well; perhaps it will help propel my tweets into several more timelines:

> BeckIsALib: #GlennBeck said, "We should save the resources that we have left." Has he some concern about the #environment?

I then followed quickly with this:

> BeckIsALib: According to a #GlennBeck quote on the #environment, "People are secondary to the Earth and animals." Seems odd for him to say.

By the way, these are real quotes. As I mentioned, I'm not going to make anything up. There is the question of context, of course, but he's never bothered with it, so why should I?

I've decided to make an adjustment to my method: I'm going to publicly thank anyone who follows me in the hopes that I can draw some extra attention. I hesitated at first, wondering if I might be breaking one of my rules, but follower thanking is pretty standard behavior in the Twitterverse and I don't think it really qualifies as pushing a point of view. So I've just sent this:

> BeckIsALib: @Kimravenscroft Thanks for the follow.

As I see it, I'm just being polite. I certainly don't want to risk losing followers just because they think me rude. I can't afford to. Even though it's only day three (and I know how these things can take time—I'm not Charlie Sheen, after all) I'm already getting a little bit nervous about whether this will work.

03 80

As we head into the first weekend, it's happened: I've lost my only follower. My guess is that @Kim saw my "thank you," took one look at what her auto-follow routine had done and thought, "uh oh." Given her pro-Beckian stance she probably shut me down faster than you can say "cognitive dissonance."

It hurts to be alone. Still, I had to put at least one tweet out there today and hope that I might soon replace @Kim with someone more forgiving:

BeckIsALib: 2007 #GlennBeck quote: "Global warming is what's causing the superfires in California." Clearly a strange thing to say. #environment

That single tweet looks as lonely on the page as I felt when I sent it out.

Michael Charney

WEEK TWO:
LACKING KLOUT

Back in 1970 Mrs. Loftus, my seventh-grade math teacher, first taught me about the dangers of social networking.

Mrs. Loftus and I both spent our days at John Burroughs Junior High School (now John Burroughs Middle School), she as faculty and I as student. John Burroughs (or JB, as we called it) is a beautiful brick building nestled on McCadden Place between Wilshire Boulevard and Sixth Street, in the Hancock Park section of Los Angeles. Many of you are probably familiar with the school, though you may not realize it; its grandeur—and proximity to Hollywood— led to frequent appearances in movies and television shows including *Pleasantville*, *Pretty in Pink*, *Teen Wolf*, and *Family Matters*. It was quite lovely as junior high schools go, set as it was in an upper middle class residential neighborhood. There were plenty of trees, several large grassy areas, and a pretty decent field in which I sat more than once as wet morning grass soaked through the green and gold shorts we wore in gym class (and which we only occasionally remembered to take home for laundering).

I was twelve years old in the seventh grade, the third youngest in my class. I was still on the short side of puberty and hadn't a clue as to what it was all about; nevertheless, I was starting to show some mild interest in girls. Well, just one girl, actually. Her name was Miri Day. (What a great name. It's real, too. I'm hoping that if she ever reads this she doesn't mind.) Miri was quite beautiful in a twelve-year-old sort of way. She had skin that tended toward olive and pitch-black hair cut into a longish Prince Valiant pageboy so that, when she leaned forward, you could just see the skin on the back of her neck. She was thin but not too much so, and had athletic arms. Miri and I shared Mrs. Loftus' math class.

Mrs. Loftus was a hard, hard woman. Red-haired and middle-aged, she spoke with a faintly leftover Irish accent and looked rather like an overworked washerwoman, a cartoon Carol Burnett, though not quite as attractive.

As a teacher she seemed steeped in a pedagogy born from a Victorian orphanage: drill, drill, slap a wrist (you could do that then), drill, embarrass publicly, then drill some more. Every day she would begin class by randomly calling on a few students and lashing questions at them. Each, when his or her turn came, would rise to a crisp military stance and loudly shout back the answer. "Janice Walker! What's the decimal equivalent of 3/8ths?" Janice, who was quite tall, knocked her knee on the desk's underside as she leapt up and barked out "Point-3-7-5" as quickly as she could. A stern nod sent her back to her seat while the rest of us sweated, wondering if we were going to be called on next and how long today's torture would last.

And God help you if you were wrong. Mrs. Loftus had raised public humiliation to an art form. With carefully scripted glaring expressions, dismissive gestures, and lip curls, she was like some mutant out of the X-Men comics that could wither your limbs from twenty feet away. Legs turned to jelly and spines cracked under the pressure. Mrs. Loftus was not to be trifled with, yet every once in a while someone tried.

Social networks in 1970 operated like this: A boy would slowly and carefully rip a small piece of paper out of a notebook and while pretending to do multiplication exercises scribble a few words onto this tiny scrap, then fold it into the smallest possible package, but certainly no larger than what could effectively disappear inside his fist. Then, carefully, while the teacher's back was turned, he would surreptitiously glide his hand forward or backward and pass the note to his nearest desk-neighbor, who would then pass it to the next nearest connection, and so on, until the note reached its destination. Any one of those connections might decide to read the note so one needed to be careful what was written on it. There wasn't any security back then. Sending a direct message might have made more sense but that was very, very chancy. It meant either leaving your seat or attempting to toss the note while Mrs. Loftus wasn't looking. Neither was worth the risk.

Eventually, that note passed from me to Miri Day. While it wasn't a love note exactly, it was certainly a *like* note. I had been lucky so far; my words had gone unread and, given that Miri and I had exchanged a few odd glances now and then, I was thinking that perhaps by the following Tuesday or so she and I might be holding hands or kissing cheeks or something. But as Miri opened the note to read my sparkling prose, Mrs. Loftus began to turn around.

I'm going to skip ahead a bit now. It's just too painful and embarrassing to recall. But I will say that the bench outside any principal's office is just as hard and uncomfortable as you remember it. I will say, also, that tears did nothing to establish me as an apt suitor in Miri's eyes.

Most importantly, through our extremely simplistic, very slow, and highly insecure seventh-grade version of tweeting and linking, I learned that, once an idea is out there, *it's out there*. Everybody—and I mean everybody—now knew about my infatuation with a girl. My friends looked at me funny, as if I had somehow betrayed not just them but the entire male pre-teen demographic. In the meantime, Miri's friends swarmed her with giggles, each punctuated with a glance in my direction. What was I doing at the time? Attempting to eat my lunch while melting into the concrete steps on which I sat, alone. It wasn't until several days later that the furor died down, superseded, no doubt, by some equally distracting blunder committed by someone else with early stage hormone rage.[3]

ᣥ ᣦ

It's been about a week since I began this experiment and I'm getting a little depressed. I shouldn't be: a week isn't such a long time. However, in the Twittersphere, where messages travel at light speed, a week feels like an eternity.

I have now accumulated two additional followers…sort of. The first—@SherriScoop—came and went so fast that I didn't even have a chance to discover anything about her. When I went to look, I was rewarded with a "suspended profile notice" and an invitation to return to my own profile instead, an exceedingly unhelpful option.

The third follower is real and has stuck around now for a couple of days. @BeAPatriot comes from Portland, Oregon, has more than 8,000 followers, and has scripted some 10,000 tweets. @BeAPatriot calls himself a "news/views service for all Patriots who Love Freedom" and adds a bit of Latin for class—*Veritas, Vos Liberabit*—which means essentially "the truth will set you free."

Truth. Such an interesting word, best defined, perhaps, as a cherry-picked series of unsupported and out-of-context claims that

---

[3] Miri and I did finally have a very short and highly platonic romance. It included some cheek kissing and a very long game of Monopoly on her living room floor while her mother no doubt smiled to herself from where she stood making lemonade in the kitchen.

provide the façade of a logical foundation for what I already believe. Call me a cynic but that's how I feel.

A rapid review of @BeAPatriot's website suggests that he is decidedly right wing. My first clue is the prominent use of the word "Patriot," so effectively co-opted and redefined so as to mean "one who never questions, or else you're one of *them*." He's written a lot of stuff about eliminating the Federal Reserve and bringing back the gold standard, along with the occasional diatribe about a conspiracy theory regarding the recent economic crisis, said crisis manufactured, in his worldview, by terrorists and/or hostile nations. Clearly no fan of the current administration, he's also written tweets like these:

BeAPatriot: REPEAL OBAMACARE: GOP raises new questions about healthcare reform - The Hill (blog).

BeAPatriot: SOCIALISM ALERT: Cuba inches towards market socialism | Cubaverdad.

He's my perfect audience.

ᇮ ᇮ

So that's it: one week, one follower. Well, technically three followers, but with two gone it's still a bit lonely out here. Talk about plodding along. Conditioned as I am (along with everyone else suffering from Twitterddiction) to getting what I want NOW, I find myself fighting the urge to go back and adjust my self-imposed rules. But not yet. First I'm going to ramp up the number of tweets, going from just two or three a day to eight or ten. I also plan to add a few more hash tags here and there in order to cast a wider net.

Today's first burst reads like this:

BeckIsALib: Said #GlennBeck: "The wealthy normally attain their largesse via human misery, corporate plundering, and the raping of the #environment."

BeckIsALib: #GlennBeck on the bailout: "The $700 billion that you're hearing about now is not only...necessary, it is also not nearly enough." #Finance

I followed those with some straight-up commentary just to mix it up a little. I need a reaction and at this point I don't care where it comes from: right or left, it's all the same to me.

BeckIsALib: The number of #GlennBeck #liberal statements is amazing. When I dig in I see many things that convince me he's just acting! It's scary!

BeckIsALib: Is #GlennBeck for real? Is he betraying the #conservative and #TeaParty principles he espouses? He's said too many #liberal things!

Later on today I'll tweet a few more. In the meantime I've decided to amuse myself by checking out some of @BeAPatriot's followers. Here are a few sample tweets, along with their self-described TwitterBlurbs:

HoldtheLine: Media Matters plots "guerrilla warfare and sabotage" against Fox.

This comes from a patriot in San Diego whose bio tells us that he is at the "home of the San Diego Tea Party."

GraceofGod: Orlando Sentinel reporter Scott Powers stuffed in closet at Bill Nelson shindig.

This one comes from a woman named Shirley, whose bio tells us that she's a "❀ Conservative ❀ Libertarian ❀ Registered Nurse ❀ Born American ~ Southern by Grace of God ❀ End Apathy ❀ No Political Correctness ❀ I Stand with Israel ✿."

Based on all those cute icons I gather that Shirley doesn't mind a little attention now and then.

And there's a lovely winner from someone who claims to predict politics, with a bio that says he has "political instinct based on facts. Understands the human mind, PR, polling, and campaigns." He offers this *bon mot*:

KnowstheScore: We voted for David Palmer, we got Charles Logan, where's Jack Bauer?

ᎧᏳ ᏵᎧ

From today's first wave comes a new follower, @Ronkowski, a humorist with a decent following and a decidedly absurdist bent. He has, for example, tweeted about the poor in Minnesota (for whom having cash in their pockets could soon become a crime) and about God's supposed illiteracy. Politically he lives on the left; recent tweets clearly support unions and the efforts of the Democrats to defeat the recently passed anti-collective-bargaining legislation in Wisconsin. Still, I'm sure he's just reading my entries as humor.

Time for my second wave of the day, another boxer's combination of quotes and commentary:

BeckIsALib: "I've made lots of money making fun of me," says #GlennBeck. Makes you wonder if he's serious about anything he says.

BeckIsALib: Guess who wrote a blurb for #GlennBeck's book? Jon Stewart! Now if that isn't liberal, I don't know what is!

That last one is a favorite of mine. It's the straight-up truth, too. I didn't have to twist or cherry-pick anything. The quote graces the paperback edition of Beck's *Arguing With Idiots*: "Finally! A guy who says what people who aren't thinking, are thinking!"

I followed that one up with another aimed at the environmentalists:

BeckIsALib: #GlennBeck: "If we could all get along together...we would leave a smaller carbon footprint." Money must be why he pretends he's #conservative.

I'm realizing these posts could quickly become repetitive. Though I've collected a sizeable list of Beckian outrageousness, I know I'll need to mix it up a bit to keep things fresh. I expect to be sending out hundreds and hundreds of tweets, and the key to effective tweeting is to write what others find interesting.

∽ ∾

Saturday morning garners two more followers, a woman named @ShelleyN33 and some guy named @Kyle6489. At first I got a bit of a thrill when I saw the email informing me that "@Kyle6489 is now following you on Twitter!" but then I went and looked at his Twitter profile and my radar clicked on. @Kyle has 118 followers, is following 754 tweeps, but has himself only tweeted a couple of times.

He's also got that stupid default egg logo that Twitter provides for you, along with a strange http link in his bio that I ain't clickin' on. And his tweets seem a little bizarre:

> Kyle6489: Start making money today by answering on-line surveys. Get PAID $25 - $75 a survey.

and

> Kyle6489: I got a party bus.

Really. I'm not making this stuff up.

@ShelleyN33 at least has a photo rather than another rancid egg, along with a bio line that includes her name. But she, too, has some odd tweets:

> ShelleyN33: You can Make $5000 per Month. Get paid $80/min to take online surveys at home.

It's pretty clear that I'm having my first encounter with Twitter-spam, but then realize it doesn't really matter. Even if Kyle and Shelley are real people, I doubt they're my target audience.

Before I tweet today, I'm going to dig a bit more into how I can effectively search the Twitterverse. It seems I haven't made it easy for others to find me, and if I don't soon figure it out then this will never work.

Basic hash tag searches haven't done the trick but, as you would expect, there are lots of tools, apps, and advice to help me do a better job of it. I decided to start with an expert, and I found a blog called *The Confidential Resources: Sources and Methods for the Investigator*, run by a Canadian firm, McEachin & Associates, Ltd., and edited by one

Richard McEachin. The site's home page hosts a picture of the late Jeremy Brett in his role as Sherlock Holmes.[4] Perfect.

McEachin devotes quite a bit of real estate to meta-searching techniques, offering pages of advice to the investigative professional. Back in February 2011 he posted a blog entry called "Twitter Searching" where he says that:

> This Twitter thing has become a necessity to the connected. It is also an evolving search problem for Investigators.
>
> Searching Twitter isn't as straightforward as I would like. Content disappears in a short time in many search facilities and search results differ depending on which search facility you use.

Not very helpful. All of this I already knew.[5]

The site does, however, provide a list of eighteen "useful, Twitter-related sites." While several look promising, I learned quickly to take care. One link warns me that the advertised app is good for "finding pics of genitalia and sex acts." No thanks. Another one, called "twitjobsearch" sounds rather like a gag site erected by Eric Idle.

The site that seems most promising is one called "Followerwonk," which claims to "search Twitter bios for a term or user name." I did a quick search on bios that contain "Glenn Beck" and was immediately rewarded with a list of 330 Twitter @names, along with their owners' real identities, geographic locations, and the

---

[4] The definitive Sherlock Holmes, Jeremy Brett, nailed the role for nearly ten years in a series of films for Granada Television in the United Kingdom. The shows were telecast here in the States as part of the "Mystery" series on PBS. If you're a true Holmesian and haven't seen these, then I strongly recommend that you put them in your Netflix queue immediately.

[5] Just for the record, the first draft read, "No shit, Sherlock."

number of tweets, followers, and friends each has. Compared to the half-a-million new Twitter accounts registered each day 330 may not seem like all that many, but it's 326 more than I knew about a few minutes ago. Since the people on this list actually put the phrase "Glenn Beck" in their bios, they are probably of more interest to me than, say, @Kyle.

My strategy is simple. I plan to review the tweets from this small but relevant list in the hopes of finding additional interesting hash tags. If I use those tags in my tweets, then—in theory—I should show up on a few more timelines.

One of the hash tags, "#conservative," is one I've already been using. Others, though, are acronyms I would never otherwise have known about. "#tcot" is very popular; it stands for "Top Conservatives on Twitter" and would seem to indicate a demographic of interest. Another, "#p2," is apparently the equivalent badge of honor for progressives. There's also "#sgp" (which stands for "Smart Girl Politics") and "#ocra" (which stands for "Organized Conservative Resistance Alliance"). The former seems a stretch for me, while the latter makes me wonder if I should be nervous about who and what is out there.

Other common tags used by Beck's fans include "#GOP" and "#TeaParty," so I'll continue to use those. Today I'll pepper my tweets appropriately. I send this:

BeckIsALib: #Glennbeck said: "The #TeaParty people, they are coming out of the woodwork. It's...a little dangerous" #GOP Why would he say this?

Quickly followed by:

BeckIsALib: Not a #TeaParty idea, but #GlennBeck said it: "The poorest are being hit by inflation harder than anybody else." Could it all be an act?

And then:

BeckIsALib: #GlennBeck said "There is no constitutional argument over whether Muslims have the right to practice their religion." #ocra #tcot Liberal?

Perhaps with these new tags my follower count will rise. Some. Just a bit. Maybe.

C8 80

I need some Klout.

In the Twitterverse there are untold ways to find out what kind of influence you're having, the most common being, of course, the number of followers you have and the number of tweets you tweet. But real influence is measured by more than just those two statistics, and people always want to know how they're doing compared to others. Coming along to satisfy that need is a little company called Klout, Inc.

Founded in 2008, Klout, a technology startup based in San Francisco, calls itself "the standard for influence," and claims to measure your online status through the use of a complex algorithm that takes into account more than twenty-five variables. The system generates a score ranging from one to one hundred. According to their website, this number "is a measure of your overall influence on the web," with higher scores indicating "a wider and stronger sphere of influence."

My Klout is ten.

Just to put that in perspective, @GlennBeck's Klout is seventy-one. In one sense that's encouraging: Beck is only seven times more influential than I am (assuming the score is linear rather than, say, logarithmic, like an earthquake's Richter ranking). Just to add to my Twitter-envy I checked Charlie Sheen's Klout: ninety-four. (As I write this, Sheen has just gone through an intensely hyperbolic and very public meltdown, during which he promptly broke every Twitter record for followers accrued in the shortest possible time span.) Lady Gaga has a Klout score of ninety-one, pretty much putting to shame Sarah Palin's anemic fifty-three; Justin Bieber hits the magic one hundred, at which point Klout helpfully informs me that "you can't get any more influential than this." Barack Obama, by the way, has a Klout score of only twenty-three. Guess he's got better things to do. Rachel Maddow's score, she of the liberally bent MSNBC, is a mere forty-two. I thought it might be higher, but maybe it's just that no one actually watches her network.

Klout isn't the only way to measure social networking influence. *The New York Times Magazine*, in an article in the March 27, 2011 issue entitled "A Better Way to Measure Twitter Influence," cites a comment by Twitter co-founder Evan Williams, who says that a large following doesn't necessarily translate into influence. The Times then went to another influence peddler, Twitalyzer, which came back with a very different perspective. They, too, issue scores from one to one-hundred, but by their ranking Lady Gaga isn't quite so influential, topping out with a score of only forty-one. The Bieb is still up there at sixty-seven, but not as far up as with Klout. Glenn Beck has a Twitalyzer score of 59.8 percent, putting him in the ninety-ninth percentile of all influencers.

My impact score under Twitalyzer is 0.1 percent, a ranking that has me orbiting the Twitterverse somewhere out near Neptune. I think I'll stick with my Klout score. It's low, but at least it's an integer.

According to Klout.com, there are a few ways to goose my Klout score. The first is frighteningly obvious but undeniably difficult: write interesting and provocative tweets. The problem is that what one tweep finds interesting is dross to another. Still, I think I've done reasonably well so far in that respect; I've at least tried to be provocative.

Any of the other recommended techniques would mean breaking my own rules in order to build a following, and I'm not ready to do that...yet.

At latest check I'm up to six followers. That's plus three from yesterday, or, phrased optimistically, a 100 percent increase from yesterday. There. Now I feel better. Maybe I just need more time.

Two of my three new followers, @GoodGovPlease and @OutofmyWallet, appear to be organizations (though sometimes it's hard to tell). Both have large followings, numbering in the many thousands. @GoodGovPlease is essentially a collection of tweets (and referent blog postings) that intersect global and national politics with Christianity while at the same time peppering in some entries on technology, finance, and the odd sports item. In my quick perusal I found it to be remarkably even-handed, covering items from across the right-to-left spectrum. I'm hoping that there's a real person behind the decision to follow me and not just an auto-routine running in the background.

@OutofmyWallet is a bit different, appearing to have only one purpose: to publicize any news at all, from anywhere at all, that might impact the American taxpayer. The tweets are clearly driven by an agenda: taxes bad, tax cuts good. Like any purely binary statement, the arguments are mind-numbingly facile, but that's what seems to pass for intelligent debate these days.

My third new follower is @SeeMeNow, a run-of-the mill tweeter who offers comments about sports one minute and Russian science fiction the next. There's a picture of a dashing red sports car on his

Twitter page and the photo he has of himself reminds me a bit of Rhys Ifans in *Notting Hill*. You know the guy: thin, blond, bit of a slob. Probably a fun guy to know, but not a leader of men. It doesn't surprise me that @SeeMeNow has a Klout score of only nineteen; still, I'll take what I can get.

附 附

When it comes to social interaction I've always preferred a bit of distance. I have a few close friends; even those I reach out to infrequently. They know me. (The nice thing about close friends is that they do know you—and like you anyway. But I'm there for them and they're there for me, whenever needed.) I've moved around the country a bit so I see these people only a few times a year, if that. Most don't live near me and visiting requires that I plan a trip of some sort: to New Jersey, to Los Angeles, to Oakland, to Schenectady.

I'm also not that much of a phone person. When I spend too long on the phone, my elbow starts to hurt. I recently bought myself a headset (the kind customer service reps commonly wear), but even that isn't great; no matter how I adjust the volume, after about twenty minutes there's this tiny little ringing in my ear and it really drives me nuts. So I call family now and then to catch up, but friends not so often. It really is the electronic world that offers connection. For someone like me it's nearly ideal: I no longer feel guilty for being out of touch and when I do get together with friends, I feel as if we've been keeping up with each other all along.

Social networking also allows me to keep in touch with others not quite as close to me: those people with whom I've glided through various portions of my life. In the old days we would have inevitably lost touch, but not so anymore. Several years ago my wife and I knew a wonderful woman, Christine, who came to our house to walk our dog while we were at work. She was great; she is great. We "see" her every day now on Facebook and share the occasional back-and-forth in a friendly, glad-to-know-you sort of way.

The same holds true for people I've worked with in the past. Those of us who have spent twenty-five or so years in the workforce remember the days when people you worked with came and went. We pretty much knew that, once gone, we would likely not cross paths again. That's all changed now. Up until the end of 2010 I worked for Thomson Reuters, a company with a huge global footprint. I managed a team of people based just outside of Tel Aviv in Israel. I've been fortunate to travel there many times and to see much of the country. It's a beautiful land with deserts that defy description, is more green than it's often given credit for, has a beautiful coastline, and a culture and people filled with life and energy and wit. I have many friends there—all of whom are people I've worked alongside. We stay connected the new-fashioned way: through email and Facebook and Linked-In, through tweets and direct mess-ages and virtual events, through posted photos and shared links. It's how it's all done, nowadays.

So I'm still an island, but floating among myriad other islands. And it works just fine.

୦୫ ୨୦

I fire a twin barrage of tweets on this Sunday afternoon. Several are repeats (cast with additional hash tags in the hopes of hooking more followers), and a few are new.

BeckIsALib: Regarding #SarahPalin, a #GlennBeck quote: "I don't know if she can lead." Do we know what he REALLY thinks? #tcot #TeaParty #GOP

BeckIsALib: #GlennBeck was raised by Democrats. How conservative can he really be? He's a great actor, but hurts the #teaparty and #conservative causes.

This last tweet is insidiously Beckian, mostly because it relies on the same guilt-by-association rhetoric that Beck loves to use. If you hang around with people who hold certain beliefs, then you must of course share those beliefs. Wasn't that the entire logical framework behind the Obama and Reverend Wright argument, or the connection between ACORN and the Clintons simply because both are from Arkansas?[6] So by Beck's own logic, if he grew up with Democrats, then he must be one. QED.

∛ √

Today is the last day of the second week and I'm working hard at keeping my spirits elevated. I'm down to five followers (though the loss was only @Kyle, he of the party bus), and it's now pretty clear that a single idea can't surreptitiously float to success, but instead will need help.

I have no "mentions," which means that not one single person in the Twitterverse is interested in responding to any of my tweets. Obviously, that also means that no one has retweeted me. Basically, @BeckIsALib is the Twitter equivalent of a grain of sand on a vast, vast beach.

Starting tomorrow one of my rules will have to go. Ah well.... Given the nearly 150 *million* tweets generated on any given day,[7]

---

[6] Stephen Zunes, Chair of the Mid-Eastern Studies program at the University of San Francisco (and contributor to *The Huffington Post*) calls this the "cootie" effect.

[7] As of this writing, in March 2011. For all I know it could be a googol per day by now.

should it really surprise me that my measly thirty or so have gotten lost in the Twitterverse?

Much as I hate to break my rules, it's time to admit that my original plan isn't working. It's time to market.

WEEK THREE:
WELCOME TO THE PARTY

G lenn Beck calls what he does "the fusion of entertainment and enlightenment," and he produces his content through his own entertainment company, Mercury Radio Arts, which he named after Orson Welles' Mercury Theater.[8] Welles, you may remember famously aired *War of the Worlds* back in 1938, a radio play based on the classic H.G. Wells novel in which Martians invade Earth. When the show was first broadcast, havoc ensued: panicked people fled and there were numerous reports from listeners who claimed to have smelled poison gas or to have witnessed flashing lights in the distance. Local police were swamped with phone calls. Thousands of people suddenly convinced themselves that fiction was reality.

Beck started in radio as a teenager, a career he began pining for years earlier when his mother gave him *The Golden Years of Radio* as an eighth birthday present. He got his first paying job at a station in

---

[8] For biographical material on Glenn Beck I am greatly indebted to the work of Alexander Zaitchik (both his Salon.com articles and his book, *Common Nonsense: Glenn Beck and the Triumph of Ignorance*) and Dana Milbank's book, *Tears of a Clown: Glenn Beck and the Tea Bagging of America.*

Seattle where he spent his weekends, often overnight. After some additional forays as a run-of-the-mill song spinner (first in Utah and later in Washington, D.C.), Beck eventually found a gig in 1983 as the morning show host on Corpus Christi's KZFM. His show was small and rather ordinary, perhaps even a tad infantile. There was Beck himself, along with a strange, imaginary Muppet-voiced character named Clydie Clyde, and a newsreader. This was during the nascent days of the "morning zoo" phenomenon, and Beck quickly found himself both successful and popular. While he certainly engaged in some over-the-top behavior in the name of competition (including once gluing shut a competitor's front doors), at this point he was still just another shock-jock wannabe, a pot-smoking, rock-and-roll-loving kid thrilled to be doing what he loved. He hadn't yet enrobed himself in the malicious arrogance that would later emerge.

His ability to compete effectively in a tough market drew the attention of WKRA in Louisville, Kentucky, and Beck left Corpus Christi to join the station in 1985. WKRA suffered from a stagnant format with poor demographics, and the owners hoped that Beck could turn around the ailing station with a fresh, zoo-oriented approach. It was here that Beck first began to evolve a specific persona; the first incarnation—"Captain Beck" of "Captain Beck and the A Team!"—was for the most part a copycat version of the day's typical morning jocks. These were the times when Scott Shannon was establishing himself in the genre, when Don Imus was quite famous for his loud-mouthed behavior (along with his equally famous irascibility), and when Howard Stern was being, well, Howard Stern.

It was in Louisville where Beck's first edgy shadows sharpened. His tenure began as expected, with standard zoo fodder built into a show peppered with skits, humor, and music. The formula included a bit of childishness, a rotating ensemble of characters and bits, and an occasional dip into the fringes of bad taste including, according to

Kathy Lincoln, Beck's former newsreader, a "really funny black guy character."

For Beck, though, it was just a short hop from bad taste to cruelty. Always a fierce competitor, Beck took aim at the Louisville market. *MediaMatters for America*, a liberal-leaning online newsmagazine, tells of Beck's obsession with Liz Curtis, an "obese host of an afternoon advice show" on another station. Curtis was "a frequent target of Beck's," *MediaMatters* reports. "It was no secret in Louisville that Curtis, whom Beck had never met and with whom he did not compete for ratings, was overweight. And Beck never let anyone forget it."

Beck continued to target Curtis for two years, but with Curtis refusing to rise to the bait Beck wasn't getting the attention he wanted. *MediaMatters* goes on to write that "despite the constant goading, Curtis never responded. But being ignored only seemed to fuel Beck's hunger for a response." His "attacks escalated and grew more unhinged," and a colleague of Curtis', Terry Meiners, tried to intervene, but to no avail. By this time the Beckian ego enjoyed full flower. Meiners remembers a morning where he walked into Beck's office "which was filled with plaques, letters, and news clippings – 'a shrine to all that is Glenn Beck.' "

Beck, however, had not yet figured out how to captivate the Louisville audience. Floundering in the ratings, he tried on new garb, that of a jingoistic loudmouth, version 1.0. Shortly after the 1986 U.S. bombing of Libya, Beck shifted his tactics, choosing to pray on the air and then play song parodies about Muammar Gadhafi and the Libyan people. Some biographers see this as the turning point for Beck, the watershed mark where the real Beck emerged. I tend to think the opposite—that Beck was just looking for any path to ratings success—but only Beck truly knows. Was it an act or was he being serious? It's hard to tell, but what we do know is that he hung up on many of his callers whose vitriol and violent rhetoric Beck felt went too far.

Despite his best efforts, Louisville never panned out for Beck. The ratings remained lackluster and Beck ended up unemployed when the station's owners decided to return to the previously anemic but relatively safe format. Broken and now heavily into drugs and alcohol (having graduated well beyond pot), Beck claimed to have considered suicide but managed to pull himself through.

Finally another opportunity emerged. Beck took his persona and moved to Phoenix to host Y95's "Morning Zoo," yet another common sort of drive time craziness populated by insanity and a shortage of social mores (and, in this case, a rented mascot named Zippy the Chimp). Still, what Beck did there broke even those loose boundaries of taste.

Apparently comfortable continuing the pick-on-the-competition model, Beck turned his sights on Bruce Kelly, an old friend from Washington, D.C. but now his rival on KZZP. Kelly was good at his job and his ratings were high, driven in part by a wickedly targeted sense of what made a good publicity stunt. He once convinced John McCain to dive into a pool of chocolate and, on another occasion, drove a steamroller over thousands of Milli Vanilli records after it came out that the duo hadn't done their own singing. Kelly knew how to get attention and the fans ate it up. Beck—as he should have—went after him. Competition is, after all, competition.

Kelly dared to mock Beck's annual (and apparently sacred) *War of the Worlds* Halloween homage to his hero, Orson Welles. Reacting with a personal animosity outsized for the slight, Beck woke up one morning and saw Hyde in the mirror. Alexander Zaitchik, writing for Salon.com, reports that Beck:

> got his revenge with what may rank as one of the cruelest bits
> in the history of morning radio. "A couple days after Kelly's

wife, Terry, had a miscarriage, Beck called her live on the air and says, 'We hear you had a miscarriage,' " remembers Brad Miller, a former Y95 DJ and Clear Channel programmer. "When Terry said, 'Yes,' Beck proceeded to joke about how Bruce [Kelly] apparently can't do anything right—about how he can't even have a baby."

"It was low class," says Miller, now president of South Carolina's Open Stream Broadcasting. "There are certain places you just don't go."

The friendship never recovered. For the first time the public saw vividly the persona that had taken over Glenn Beck. A career that began with humor and spirited (if childish) pranks had since devolved into bad taste and then into cruelty.

He was just getting started.

 C3 &0

I'm sitting here early on a Sunday morning thinking about the recent week's effort. It's very quiet. One of my two dogs, Kayda, a nine-year-old standard poodle, lies on her bed next to me in my upstairs office, softly snoring and occasionally running in place as she chases after a dream-generated squirrel. The other, Zoe, a rescued mutt with an abundance of herding instinct, mottled fur, and blue eyes, is downstairs lying on the couch which, fortunately, is the same color as her fur. She sheds. I have a cup of coffee in front of me and am still in my robe. It's barely seven o'clock. My wife just left, heading off to Peterborough where she'll meet up with a friend and then head over to the Episcopalian church on Concord Street.

Week Two ended with a whole lot of "Tuesday, nothing."[9] No traction, no new followers, no increased Klout. For the last few days I've been trying out a new strategy but have resisted the urge to check my stats. While I didn't *want* to break my rules, it rapidly became clear that I had to. "Tuesday, nothing," just wasn't where I wanted to be.

Twitter is enormous. I knew that, but didn't anticipate how easily my tweets would be swallowed up, digested, and tossed aside. Thinking that I could just drop in a few tweets here and there was, as Julia Roberts might say, a "Big mistake. Big. Huge!" Twitter requires that you work the system if you want to be heard. I decided to do just that and I don't feel bad about it in the least.

Okay, maybe I feel a little bad about it, but the goal of this exercise (or at least one of them) is to seed an idea into the Twitterverse in a way that gets some people somewhere to imagine that idea as possibility. While I hoped that a solitary meme dropped into the marketplace of ideas would take off, the truth is that it never had a real chance. Such memes are rare and, when they do take root, require time to grow.

On the other hand, new and strange concepts are marketed all the time. (That's pretty much all Glenn Beck does, isn't it?) What's wrong with pushing the idea, working the system, and trying to build something instead of hoping it just builds itself?

So I went ahead—as I said, feeling a little bad about it—and broke the rules, and now, in the middle of Week Three, I decide to check my stats. Things have changed quite a bit. My follower count sits at thirty-five, up from six, and my Klout is up to twenty-eight.

---

[9] Very obscure reference here to "Nothing" by the Fugs. Other songs by the band include "Where is My Wandering Jew?" and "The Ballade of the League of Militant Agnostics." They're an acquired taste.

I've been mentioned in others' tweets a total of seventeen times, and have had two retweets.

If I'd had a bit more coffee, I'd feel positively giddy.[10]

Drilling down into my Klout score reveals that I am now "influential to a tightly formed network that is growing larger" and someone who is "more likely to have their message amplified than the average person." I have a "strong true reach!" So what does it all mean? I have no clue. On the one hand, there's that giddiness. On the other, I feel a bit like Navin Johnson when the new telephone books arrived, naively excited at seeing his name in print.[11]

I fueled my growth with just a few changes. First I started following other Twitterers.[12] For the last three days I've targeted about forty to fifty people each day, mostly by doing searches on interesting tags and phrases ("glennbeck" being the obvious one, but I also searched on "teaparty," "conservative," and even "libtard"). I found an interesting mix of people from the right side of the aisle and I was pleased to discover only a few that were frightening.[13] What struck me most was that, even though some views were extreme (birther claims, 9/11 conspiracy theorists) and some mere parroting (liberal media complaints, Obamacare misconceptions), the overall tone of the conversation was surprisingly polite. I didn't really expect that—which obviously says more about me than about

---

[10] Always thought this was a strange phrase. Is it possible to be "negatively giddy?" Turns out that "giddy" comes from the same root Germanic word as "God," and originally referred to being "possessed by a God."

[11] Steve Martin, as a poor black child, only white, in *The Jerk,* one of the "50 greatest comedies of all time," according to *Premier Magazine.*

[12] Twitterer or Tweeter: the jury is still out. But not twits.

[13] "Frightening" includes things like "**Obama** Kill The Elderly Policy Exposed - **Nazi** Obamacare Healthcare Reform Euthanasia Genocide." And that's one of the few I'm comfortable repeating.

those tweeting. Turns out I, too, can be a biased, judgmental jackass. Who knew?

Rather than the stereotypes drilled into my head by others, I discovered instead a large community of decent people who just happened to disagree with me (sometimes strongly) on a number of issues. @RonWitherspoon, for example, is a reasonably gentle looking middle-aged man from the Southwest. He loves hockey and football, reads philosophy, and listens to Shostakovich. He quotes Aristotle. This is a guy I'd want to hang out with. His tweets are thoughtful and reasoned, oriented largely around the deficit and the desire to unseat what he sees as a too-liberal agenda. He does his research and rarely, if ever, rants. He's also got a pretty droll sense of humor:

RonWitherspoon: According to Drudge, Jesse Ventura would consider joining a Ron Paul for President ticket. What could possibly go wrong?

Another follower I've grown fond of is @Escape. I've had several interesting conversations with him and, again, was surprised to realize just how pervasive my own biases are. He has an interesting, well-written blog (which he admits to being a series of "rants"), and he, too, does his homework. He's willing to engage on ideas he doesn't agree with. @Escape is strong-minded and requires a fair bit of convincing, but he too remains polite and thoughtful. I enjoy our exchanges.

Not all followers are quite so civil, particularly if they're representing a group with an agenda. That's where the Twitterverse can get really mean. Maybe it's because people can hide behind an organization and so don't feel personally responsible for what they tweet about. Anonymity is a powerful shield when one needs it to be. The Nevada Republican Liberty Caucus, for example, shouts out tweets like this:

> Nevada_RLC: NEW INFORMATION!! Massacre of 800 to 1,000 Catholics in Ivory Coast likely work of Islamists. #gop #liberty

What the tweet[14]—and the accompanying biased webpage—fail to say is that the Ivory Coast is in the middle of a horrendous civil war and that those who were slaughtered were in an overwhelmingly Muslim part of the country. The tweet could have read "Tragic loss of life in middle of Ivory Coast civil war," but that wouldn't have done as much to stir up anti-Muslim sentiment in the U.S.

In addition to building my follower list, I've also decided to change my engagement strategy. I am no longer focusing only on Beckian tweets; that will come later. I've decided to join the community; rather than just trying to communicate my ideas I am instead engaging in conversations. It turns out that talking is a good practice. When people learn about each other, they can often find common ground—which then provides an opening for them to hear what you really want to say.

Engaging in the Twittersphere means replying to tweets, retweeting others' tweets, and participating not only in the conversations I want to have, but in the conversations others want to have with me. Here's an example of a recent back-and-forth between myself and @JonDegruder, another Republican exploring the potential 2012 GOP candidates:

---

[14] As I was editing this, I realized that I had accidentally created a new expletive. I hereby christen "What the Tweet?" as the Twitterverse equivalent of "What the F**k?"

BeckisALib: Obama proves we need a Pres with real experience and brains. Who do we have for 2012? Palin: no experience; Romney: no brains. Who else?

JonDegruder: @BeckIsALib Herman Cain? Tim Pawlenty? I don't know. Herman Cain has business experience and has brains.

BeckIsALib: @JonDegruder Pawlenty, maybe. I'm keeping an eye out. Cain has no experience: business and government are very different.

JonDegruder : @BeckIsALib True - but he did say he kept his pizza chain out of bankruptcy. Pawlenty seems good, too. Will have to keep watch.

Developing relationships also helps when Friday rolls around. Fridays are special days in the Twitterverse. Referred to as "Follower Fridays" (and often abbreviated simply as "FF"), Friday has become the day when tweeters recommend others to follow. A typical Follower Friday tweet looks something like this:

HolyCow412 #FF @Kennyhertz @magirl17 @imwithyou @johdonne @clippership @taibo41 @liveordie @obamagirl8 @beckisalib @highwaves

The original tweeter, @HolyCow412, starts her tweet with "#FF" signaling a recommendation list, then follows with a bunch of Twitter @names. One of them is mine. In theory some of her followers will check me out and perhaps even choose to follow me, all based on her suggestion. The time spent in building relationships, finding new followers, and retweeting others starts to pay off when your name shows up on an #FF tweet. Such publicity invariably leads to still more followers. It's an interesting and powerful convention.

The Follower Friday habit began in 2009 with a single tweet from Micah Baldwin.[15] Now it's a vital part of Twitterquette. There are even tools (such as FollowFridayHelper, which I use) to identify quickly those you interact with most often out of the thousands and thousands of tweets that fill up your timeline.

After #FFs, retweeting is probably the most potent way to get exposed to potential followers. I've been retweeting others quite a bit lately. According to Dan Zarella, an acknowledged social media expert who applies scientific methods to social networking phenomena, retweeting creates buzz, traffic, and followers, all of which I need. Retweeting is an amplifier with the potential to raise your voice to a Spinal-Tap-level "11." Zarella also suggests that one of the easiest ways to increase your retweets is simply to ask—politely, of course. Apparently the use of the word "please" in your tweet (as in "please RT") magnifies the likelihood of a retweet by a factor of six.

So starting tomorrow I'll spend my afternoons begging.

છ ૭ૐ

Considering my tone of voice, my disdain for all things Beckian, and my general flippancy toward the abduction of such words as "patriot" and "liberty," it would only be natural for you to assume that I'm a steadfast liberal. I forgive you for coming to that conclusion; it's not true.

---

[15] Micah Baldwin is my hero. A single tweet becomes a meme becomes a convention. Wow. I'd love to do that. And from the #followfriday idea came others. There is now #musicmonday, #winewednesday, #thankfulthursday and #wkendthx. There's also something called #nopantstuesday, which apparently has something to do with the NYC subway system. I have little interest in knowing more.

I'm a Republican, and have been most of my adult life. I voted for John McCain[16], and felt then (and still feel now) that Barack Obama is in so far over his head that the weight of the water is all but crushing him. His policies are weakly constructed and inconsistent, and his inability to motivate people toward consensus means that he can't do the one thing he was truly elected to do: make us all feel better. Instead, what we have is a government more polarized than ever before and in danger of becoming a mere shadow of its former self.

The Republican Party was founded in the mid-nineteenth century on just a few fundamental principles. The party's first slogan was "free labor, free land, free men." Free labor referred to the opposition to slavery and the importance of the small businessman; free land referred to the party's opposition to a plantation system that favored the wealthy over the worker; and free men referred to the party's loathing of slavery. These platform planks outlined what is often forgotten today: that the Republican Party began as a socially open-minded, socially responsible, socially inclusive, and socially progressive assembly.

While the GOP has always taken a primary interest in the value and benefit of a strong business community, states' rights, and the power of the individual, the shift to social conservatism is relatively recent. It wasn't until well into the twentieth century that social conservatives (ironically built as much from Southern Democrats as from Republicans) had any real impact on the Republican platform and, while strongly conservative seeds were planted all through the 1960's and 1970's (particularly and shamefully with respect to civil

---

[16] I really, really wanted to say "proudly voted for John McCain," but his blatant pandering (not to mention stupidity) in choosing Sarah Palin as a running mate means that I can't in good conscience use that particular adverb. Still, the fact that I was willing to bet he'd live out his term and thereby protect us from *her* shows how much I was rooting against Obama.

rights), it wasn't until Reagan's re-election in 1984—when the GOP firmly gained the southern stronghold begun with Nixon's strategy years earlier—that true social conservatism emerged as fundamental to the party philosophy.

In contrast to the socially conservative lineage of the last three decades, the party's first victorious presidential candidate was none other than Abraham Lincoln, a man dedicated to unity, equality, and fairness. Lincoln's Republican Party formed around a fervent desire to build a coalition concerned with the human condition.

I doubt that today many would associate the GOP with those early aspirations. A June 2011 Rasmussen poll found that 39 percent of people surveyed felt that the GOP agenda was "extreme." The poll also found that 46 percent of all voters believed the average Republican in Congress is more conservative than the voters themselves are.[17]

The Republican Party has always had its extreme fringe. During the GOP's formative years, the extreme element became known as the Radical Republicans and, much like the Tea Party of today, they soon became a force in Congress. But the Radical Republicans were nothing like the Tea Partiers; the Radical Republicans of the nineteenth-century were considered so because they were *too liberal*. Early on they opposed the Kansas-Nebraska Act that would have allowed those bread-basket states to choose, upon admission to the Union, whether or not they wanted to enter as slave states or free. After the Civil War, the Radical Republicans wanted not only the abolition of slavery, but for former black slaves to have complete equality with white citizens. They were looking for ways to create an "us" out of "us and them," and to create social equality by taking the initiative needed to raise up the poorest of our poor.

---

[17] In fairness, the Democrats don't come out looking even this good; 47 percent of voters see them as extreme.

Cue the irony.

That's not to say there aren't some very real differences between mainstream Democrats and Republicans. Of course there are. Republicans are often accused of being pro-business[18] while the Democrats are pro-worker. We've also been accused of hating unions, bad-mouthing education, and ignoring the poor. None of these accusations have merit. The GOP simply has a different underlying philosophy, one based on individual rights and individual accountability. This nation has a long history of federal programs that don't do what they're supposed to, often resulting in unintended consequences. Helping people doesn't (and shouldn't) always mean giving. There are other types of help. Whether one agrees or not is beside the point; what's relevant is that the simplistic view that Republicans (even conservative Republicans) are hard-hearted leads only to cemented opinions and outsized righteousness.

Declaiming that one is a Republican used to be much simpler. Today, however, it requires qualification. I am what has been referred to pejoratively as a RINO: A Republican In Name Only. I can't tell you how much this offends me. I'm a Republican. A good, solid Republican. A Republican who believes in the basic things good, solid Republicans are supposed to believe in.

Those principles are few and, for me, well defined. First and foremost I believe in fiscal responsibility. That means we should try to stay out of debt when we can, not waste money on stupid things, and lean toward promoting private-sector over public-sector jobs. Our government hasn't been very good at this in a long time.

---

[18] To me that's not an accusation; it's laudable. Business—particularly small business—drives this country. Without it we would probably be about as successful as Burundi. (Sorry. I didn't mean to take a slap at the, I'm sure, hardworking and industrious Burundians. They probably have a very nice country. It's just that they are, relatively speaking, quite a bit poorer than we are and, unfortunately for them, the word "Burundi" sounds kinda funny.)

The only thing I know for sure about fiscal policy is that it is uproariously complex. Few people truly understand it (though everyone thinks they do), and most economic experts have about as much luck predicting the economy as I do predicting lottery numbers.

I don't even really understand what a dollar is. Think about it: I work for you and you then give me pieces of paper. I then give those pieces of paper to someone else and they give me stuff like Three Musketeers bars and Uggs. If either one of us decides that this paper really is just, well, paper, the game's up.[19] And yet we're all quite comfortable with it. Well, maybe not Ron Paul. But other than him, pretty much everybody.

Yet given this complexity (and the shibboleth on which it's based), people still feel compelled to reduce our economic planning to a series of rote idiocies. The need for a constitutional amendment to balance the budget is one such example. Just dumb. Amendments are for fundamental rights, like voting and choice and due process. They shouldn't be used to design the nuts and bolts of how we run our government. The balanced budget idea is also based on the maxim that debt is always bad. It's not. Debt is amoral. It's just a tool; it's how people choose to deploy that tool that results in good or bad.

So why do we spend so stupidly and recklessly? The obvious answer is that we spend because we have in the past. There's a huge amount of debt and commitment already out there, and no one really wants to do the hard (and politically suicidal) work necessary to re-build rather than just tinker a bit. Part of the reason is because everybody wants the problem fixed on someone else's back. Spend less on them, the mantra goes, but not on me. It seems that the days of true

---

[19] On top of which, a lot of us don't even use the paper any more: we use the *idea* of paper stored as digital signals.

national sacrifice are gone for good. Try to imagine, say, widespread gas and sugar rationing in order to make sure we win the war on terror. Not a chance. Hell, most people can't even honestly stick to odd-even lawn watering days during the slightest of droughts.

One of the most common responses to getting something is that once we have it, we really want to keep it. Recent research shows that, as a species, we are hard-wired to feel horrible when we encounter loss; the emotional response is much stronger than when we gain.[20] As a result, it's in our nature to grasp talon-like to anything we have. Unfortunately, this country has given out some pretty big prizes along the way: Medicare and Medicaid, Social Security, and enormous Defense Department contracts, just to name a few. These are not in and of themselves bad programs; they help a lot of people and they keep a lot of private-sector employees cashing paychecks every two weeks. But trying to touch any of these entitlements means that someone, somewhere, gets less of it, and most people believe that if MY representative or senator starts down that path it's a bad thing; let the other guy take the hit. So any politician that raises such specters is likely to become one of the several hundred thousand who are forced to file an unemployment insurance claim every Monday.

This country needs a little tough love, and we need it from brave public servants[21]. We're spoiled children, people. Unfortunately, we're spoiled children who get to choose new parents every few years, and so the parents are scared. Given that fiscal responsibility remains a hardened cornerstone of the GOP credo, Republicans—real Republicans—should be willing to fight that fight. Instead, what

---

[20] For a list of references see http://loss-aversion.behaviouralfinance.net, or just ask my wife what mood I was in after I sold Netflix at a 400 percent profit, only to see it double again in the next six months.

[21] Please don't laugh. I'm trying to make a serious argument here.

passes for the Republican Party today is a lot more like the odd uncle who slips his nephew an extra twenty every once in a while because he thinks that's the only way the kid will ever like him, and then admonishes that same kid to spend it wisely. Said nephew then rushes out to buy baseball cards and fantasy figurines before sheepishly returning to beg for more.

The next principle—and for me almost as important as fiscal responsibility—is national defense. That's as traditionally Republican as you can get, but I'm betting my definition is different than yours, which is probably more like the one I found in the Strategic Objectives section of the *National Defense Strategy of the United States of America, March 2005*. The document lists several objectives including securing the United States from direct attack (which gets top priority[22]), securing strategic access and global freedom, strengthening alliances, and establishing favorable security conditions.

I'm betting that if you asked most people for their definition they would come up with something similar, though I imagine it would be simplified a bit, perhaps to something like "Don't let them attack us, but if they do, kick the crap out of 'em so they know not to do it again." It's the U.S. version of Mr. Miyagi at the end of *The Karate Kid*.

I'm sorry, but I don't agree.

Traditional defense is part of it—a big part of it—but what the National Defense Strategy seems to be saying is that our strategy should target keeping us safe. I think our strategy should be about more than that; it should be about preserving and enhancing our way of life. That's different.

"How?" you ask. One simple word: *Education*.

There's nothing more important to our national defense than building a nation of intelligent, insightful, and thinking people. I

---

[22] Bet you're glad to hear that. My brain, frankly, is screaming: *as opposed to what?!??*

don't care how many bombs we have; if the next couple of generations are stupid, they'll just use them to blow things up.

I'm sorry to say that it looks like that's where we're headed. Scores from the *2009 Programme for International Student Assessment* show that the United States ranks fourteenth in reading, seventeenth in science, and twenty-fifth in mathematics. That's where we sit on a list of thirty-four developed countries. In reading we rank below Norway, Estonia, and Poland. In mathematics we're right behind Slovenia.[23] In science, we again get to look up at Estonia, and also Iceland and Canada. And of those thirty-four countries, only eight have a lower high school graduation rate than we do.

Want to destroy a way of life? Easy. Let the rest of the world get smarter than you and they'll go and figure out how to grow their way of life faster than you grow yours. I don't care how many Wal-Marts McDonalds and Starbucks we scatter across the world, the people with the brains eventually become the people with the money and the power. It's that simple.[24]

And, finally, solid Republicanism embraces the struggles and rewards of individual freedom, individual responsibility, and a universal morality encircled by mutual respect. Sadly, this last point is where I think our party has gone the most amiss. Respect seems harder and harder to find, replaced instead by undignified infighting and partisan bullying.

∽ ∾

---

[23] I bet we're behind them in geography, too, since they probably know where we are but I doubt the reverse is true.

[24] It's really not. Nothing is that simple. But I feel so strongly about the issue, believe so *vividly* that we are getting way too stupid to be the leaders of the free world, that I just wanted to make the point with a bit of flair.

Week Three has come to an end. In many ways I feel like I've gotten a fresh start. No longer just a town crier with a broken megaphone, I'm now actively engaged. I end the week with eighty followers and a Klout score of thirty-six. I've dropped more than 200 tweets. Importantly, a good number of those new followers are tweeps that I did not first follow. They somehow found me. That's a good sign. I even feel—and this is unexpected—like I've made a few friends.

And yet all that is unimportant right now. Today Glenn Beck officially announced that he is ending his show on Fox News.

Michael Charney

WEEK FOUR:
I BELIEVE IN ME

O r did he?
Depending on which headline you prefer, either Fox News parted ways with Glenn Beck or Beck parted ways with Fox. The stories emerged simultaneously, assembled from bits and pieces like a ransom note in a Raymond Chandler novel and broadcast loudly in bold Helvetica type. Beck, smartly out in front of the story, expertly managed his own version. I watched Beck interviewed by another Fox commentator, Judge Andrew Napolitano, and it sure sounded to me like it was Beck's call. I doubt, though, that it was the actual Glenn Beck talking. More than likely his persona showed up; he wore that almost-penitent, gee-golly smile on his face, spoke softly and gently, and seemed almost contrite. The guy's that good.

Press coverage wasn't much help in sorting it all out either, largely because the story's meaty flavor exposed everyone's carnivorous bias. Liberal outlets dwelt on Beck's upcoming departure (barely able to contain a self-serving "I told you so") while the more conservative voices emphasized Beck's future and the amazing opportunities now before him. NPR reported that "both parties call[ed] it a mutual agreement amid declining ratings and rumors of discord between

Beck and the network," while Fox emphasized instead that they and Beck, working together, "will team to produce a slate of projects for FOX News Channel and FOX News' digital properties."[25] Any direct reference to Beck's departure—what Fox called a "transition off of his daily program"—never even made it into the lead paragraph, relegated instead to paragraph two, only secondarily relevant. Beck's own press release only says that he looks forward "to starting this new phase of our partnership."

Sitting at the far left side of the spectrum, *MediaMatters* barely attempted objectivity, letting the event instead trigger another flurry of insults. "Conservative bloggers," they wrote, "have reacted with a mixture of sorrow, skepticism, and, of course, conspiracy theories about why his show is ending."[26]

For sheer carnival barker amusement nothing came close to Stephen Colbert's faux-conservative response. Warning everyone of the coming "Glennpocalypse," Colbert advised people to create a "Beckpack" containing "everything you need to survive in a post-Glenn world." Your Beckpack should include all the books Beck has ever written along with "a tasty helping of beef stroganoff." He went on to warn us that we should keep our Beckpack on at all times so that "we need never face our greatest fear: not knowing what to be afraid of."[27]

The Twittersphere filled quickly with typically outsized reactions. Timelines overflowed with topical tweets faster than a cuckoo dis-

---

[25] Fox likes to call itself FOX, by the way. I don't. They really shouldn't yell like that. It's not like it's an acronym for anything, although I'm sure there are plenty of people who would like it to mean "F**k Off...something."

[26] It's the "of course" that gets me.

[27] Colbert actually did this bit on the rumor rather than the announcement, but so what? It's funny.

cards the unwanted eggs from another bird's nest. The tone ran from raucous to cruel to rude, all with easily predictable slants. Here are a few of the nicer ones:

> Nofoxtoday: Now that Glenn Beck has been fired... who will take the lead on hating gays, liberals, and global warming?

> Fingall14: Glenn Beck got kicked to the curb like a dog with mange by Fox News.

Here's one from the other side:

> Cowjumpedover: No Fox News doesn't mean the Beck boogeyman is leaving liberal closets.

There were many, many more not-so-nice ones. They range from the merely snarky...

> Dumboelephant: Looks like the Tea Party will receive all of my attention now that Glenn Beck was fired like a HUGE Puss from Fox News! I WILL SURVIVE!

...to the frighteningly insane:

> GivemeaJ: Why Did Fox Terminate Glenn Beck? He was exposing his Juden Masters for the *SCUM* they are.[28]

And then there's this tweet, one of several that made me want to disinfect my computer screen after reading it:

---

[28] At this point it might help to take a deep breath and remember that the First Amendment protects you, too.

RantnRave: Glenn Beck is C**t of the Day. So now there will be
one less hateful turd floating in the toilet bowl that is Fox News.

As is often the case with such malignant speech, the lack of self-
awareness betrays the underlying irony. Who in this little morality
play is truly the hateful one?

I am convinced that we'll never be sure of the facts surrounding
Beck's departure. The left wants to believe he was fired due to low
ratings and public backlash while the right prefers the moving-on-to-
bigger-things story. Meanwhile the rest of us remain on the ropes,
pummeled with assumptions, half-truths, and spin, yet still fitting the
pieces carefully into our own personal view of what "really"
happened. We weave our own myth out of the fabric of what we
want to believe.

Facts are unimportant these days. We live in a time of instant
myth-making, a time when revisionist history happens almost before
history occurs, a time when the new model for rhetoric is to treat
everything like it's a high school term paper.

It's Saturday afternoon. The 750-word essay that Mr. Winston
assigned for your eleventh-grade U.S. history class is due on Monday
morning, third period. You find the subject—the role of the Supreme
Court—deadly dull, and after slogging through eighteen pages of
densely packed text you are no closer to getting started than before.
Your older sister suggested that you just go to the library and find an
article to copy, but a gnawing conscience eats away at you and won't
let you do it. The day's drifting away and your friends, all of whom
have either completed the assignment or were lucky enough to get
Mrs. Carfulli instead, are off playing stickball.

Sitting in front of an annoyingly blank piece of notebook paper
and with a Bic poised in your right hand, you think about it for a few
minutes, hoping that something will spring to mind. You rescan the

eighteen pages to make sure you have a basic understanding of the U.S. Supreme Court and its responsibilities, how justices are selected, and how decisions are made. If you concentrate, you can just barely remember seven of the nine current members and their appointing presidents, enough, probably, for a B+ should there be a pop quiz. Forcing your mind back to the task at hand, you refocus on getting this shitty little essay drafted so that you can get it behind you and salvage whatever's left of the weekend.

So you decide what to believe. Your brain kicks in to get-this-over-with mode and you just go with your gut and believe something. You take no time to explore facts or alternatives, or to analyze what you've read. Your brain comes up with something like "members of the Supreme Court aren't really objective when they decide cases," then you roll the idea around a little to see how it tastes before deciding that it's a reasonable mix of opinion and comprehension, just the kind of thing Mr. Winston likes. A quick review of the reading assignment reveals nothing that would disagree with your premise; the idea feels safe and solid. It sounds good and feels good, so you go with it.

You haven't done any research to support the idea and you can't verbalize where it came from. Most likely you've internalized opinions half-heard from your parents or *The Huntley-Brinkley Report*. It doesn't matter, though; you've decided.

Welcome to the birth of content-free thinking.

There's still the actual writing to do, but now it'll be a breeze. You just need to cherry-pick a couple of supporting examples and a few references, then clothe them in a bit of intellectual underwear. Seven hundred and fifty words won't even raise a sweat.

You head to the library where you find a couple of books that look like they'll serve as useful references, then you dig up two quotes buried in a microfiched magazine article.[29] Adding citations from two recent Supreme Court decisions fills nearly half of a note-book page. You fill up another half with your basic argument, taking care to use as many extra words as possible in order to meet the essay's length requirement. Then you fit in the quotes you found where they seem to belong and log all your references in classic Strunk-and-White style. A final word count takes two minutes, then you spend another ten on a quick re-read. One subject-verb agreement error and a spelling mistake require correction, and you call it your second draft. Recopying the essay onto a fresh sheet of paper finishes things off.

An idea that began as thin air now seems breathable. You've finished the paper and have now spent a couple of hours working on a convincing argument. In order to feel good about your work you need to believe it, at least a little bit. And the more you believe it, the more you believe it more.

The change isn't just in your imagination; it's in your brain. Recent discoveries in the area of neuroplasticity—the ability of the brain's neurons to change, weaken, and strengthen with time and practice—confirm that concentration on an idea can reinforce the strength of that idea in your brain. Alvaro Pascual-Leone, chief of the Beth Israel Deaconess Medical Center at Harvard University, uses the analogy of sledding down a snowy hill in winter. The first time down, he says, you create a bit of a track down the slope. The second time down it's easier and faster to use the same track, so the track gets a little deeper. Each time you ride that sled, you're reinforcing what has gone before. So, too, with the brain. Basically, the more you

---

[29] Today you just head to the internet, parked conveniently on your iPad or laptop and available while you munch on a Bacon Turkey Bravo at Panera. Back then it meant hopping on a green three-speed Stingray with an enormous sissy-bar and pedaling the four miles to the Gardner Park Library.

think about something you believe, the more that belief will strengthen over time.[30]

Once you believe something, you're also unlikely to let a little thing like *facts* get in the way, and that's where things get scary. A series of studies conducted by the University of Michigan in 2005 and 2006 revealed that facts don't change our beliefs—and can actually make our wrong beliefs even *stronger*. Our psyche doesn't like to admit error. If someone believes that Planned Parenthood is an abortion factory, telling her that PP is prohibited from using federal funding for abortions won't change her mind. She'll just nestle more deeply into her belief, perhaps arguing that "money is money" and you can't slice it up like that, or that no one can ever really be sure because they're probably messing with the books anyway. Show an anti-death penalty advocate scientific studies that support the death penalty as a deterrent and he'll respond by pointing you to a website like deathpenaltyinfo.org, which is filled with studies of the studies that prove all your points wrong. Then you dig in. You're not immune; you demonstrate the same resistance to conversation, relying instead on broadcasting the same arguments and the same "truths," as if—somehow—the fifth or sixth repetition will finally result in a changed opinion.

At heart we're all Journey fans: we won't stop believing.

By the time you hand that paper in to Mr. Winston, you'll believe what's in it almost as much as if you had personally conducted a series of extensive, scientifically valid studies. And if anyone should ask you your opinion today on the role of the Supreme Court, your truth probably won't be much different than the truth you created for yourself back in high school, regardless of the facts.

---

[30] From *The Brain that Changes Itself*, by Norman Doidge. Full disclosure: I didn't read it all. Mostly I went trolling through it in order to cherry-pick bits of data that would support what I already believed or was pretty sure I had read elsewhere.

We'll never know the Beck-and-Fox story in anything that approaches the "truth." We'll just believe what we want to, based on what we already believe and what our like-minded Twitterians believe along with us. I have faith that Beck will be around for a while, though. We have an election coming up and there's a ton of money to be made.

C3 ‰

I'm learning things about myself that I don't like. My tweets feel more conservative, and I've noticed a shift in my tone of voice. For example, I recently wrote the following:

> BeckIsALib: #tcot let's stop calling them ENTITLEMENTS and start calling them what they are: ASSISTANCE. Some may need, but no one's entitled.

I have no clue what thistle-infested corner of my brain produced that thought, but I've now spent several weeks poring over streams of tweets, most of them strongly conservative and perhaps my lurch to the right results from immersion. I prefer to think, though, that I've simply become more open-minded.

Perhaps the idea isn't so outlandish. In the current mood, pervasively bathed in austerity and concern as it is, maybe it's understandable that the thought of people taking unneeded benefits would cause others to lash out. Have I sheepishly absorbed the marketing—words like "entitlement" and "need" and "basic"—and become too accepting of these all-encompassing programs simply because they've been around for most of my life and I can't imagine any other way to be? Perhaps it's only that I'm finally willing to look more closely at my own assumptions and beliefs.

But then why did I follow that first tweet with this one?

BeckIsALib: Urge you to RT: They're not ENTITLEMENTS, they're ASSISTANCE. Changing language changes attitudes.

I know what my conscious mind was thinking at the time: controversy and originality breed retweets, and retweets breed Klout. So why not broadcast a controversial idea in an original way and ask for the retweet? The worst that will happen is nothing—just another lonely tweet cast adrift. On the other hand, if it works I build influence.

Then I remember that I never set out to change anyone's thinking about entitlements or assistance or whatever the hell I think it is right now. The idea-changing part of this experiment was supposed to be about Glenn Beck and he doesn't even appear in these tweets. So what's happening to me? And what's with all the CAPITAL LETTERS? Who the hell am I yelling at?

Here's the bit that's frightening: I started out trying to get people to change their thinking and instead it seems that people are changing mine.

The definitions are moving. I'm moving.

∛ ∵

After Glenn Beck flamed out in Phoenix[31] he surfaced again in Houston early in 1989 where, according to Alexander Zaitchik, he would "produce some of the worst radio of his career." Hired by KRBE at an extremely attractive salary and with the highest of hopes, Beck was set to take on Houston's reigning "zoo" champ, John Lander.

---

[31] Another screamingly obvious metaphor; you do the work.

Beck started out handicapped. Lander, already nationally syndicated and number one in the Houston market, was considered a zoo-keeping star, while Beck, with only himself and his odd-voiced alter ego Clydie Clyde, floundered like a local shopkeeper forced to compete with Walmart. He knew what he was up against, though, and went out of his way to be outrageous in order to garner some attention. On Beck's very first show at KRBE, Clydie Clyde asked listeners to drop some breakfast meat and a raw egg into an envelope and mail it to the station. While the Houston weather was much cooler than normal when Beck pulled the stunt, it still wasn't pretty. More importantly, it didn't help the ratings.

Never a fan of failure, the take-no-prisoners Beckian ego began looking for some tactic, some niche where Beck might stand out. With eight years of Bill Clinton ending and Texas about to seat another Bush as president, Beck saw an unfilled opening and decided to inject some good old-fashioned patriotism into his show.

Less than a month into his contract, Beck started planning an American-themed extravaganza in support of the military's fighting forces. He even managed to broadcast a week's worth of shows from an aircraft carrier, the USS Theodore Roosevelt, then patrolling the southern Mediterranean Ocean. A new—and potentially more interesting—Glenn Beck emerged.

Potential does not mean success, however. Despite the flag waving, the patriotic songs, and the on-air appearances of such heavyweights as Bob Hope, Ronald Reagan, and Mickey Mouse,[32] the Houston radio audience remained less than impressed, and the military-themed celebration did little to increase Beck's numbers. Beck ended up losing his Houston gig and, after a protracted and

---

[32] Once again, I think you're perfectly capable of inserting your own punch line. If it helps to make it funnier, add "Tina Yothers" into the mix; she, too, was a guest.

bitter severance dispute, word got out that he was hard to work with. At only twenty-six Beck's career was in trouble.[33]

With even Ronald Reagan failing to boost the ratings, it was no surprise that Beck's next move was again to a marginal station struggling in a secondary market. In 1990 Beck landed at B104 in Baltimore, again assigned to shore up a flagging Top-40 format, only this time with a partner, a jock with morning show experience named Pat Gray, someone Beck knew faintly from the days when they were both in Houston working for competing stations. Gray's arrival proved fortuitous, particularly since he was a last-minute replacement for Mike Opelka, the partner Beck originally planned on working with but who had backed out shortly before launch.

Beck and Gray buried themselves in marathon writing sessions and for a while it looked like the duo might pull it off; they had chemistry and some of their ideas were classic by zoo standards. One stunt involved a gerbil and a bank tube and another had people driving around the D.C. Beltway looking for a non-existent underground theme park named "Magicland."

Even with a solid partner and flashes of the early, zoo-possessed Beck, the ratings never spiked high enough to satisfy the station's overlords. Drinking became even more of a problem (though he remained a pro at the studio), and Beck, a self-described "borderline schizophrenic,"[34] claimed to have regularly downed drugs for ADHD. The station canceled Gray's contract after barely a year on

---

[33] I like to think of myself as a pretty fair-minded person, and while it's clear I'm not a Glenn Beck fan, I will offer appropriate kudos when they're due. I know very few people who managed to accomplish anything comparable at that age. Say what you will about the pot or the long hair, about the attitude or the mean streak, this kid was balls-to-the-wall with a nearly unparalleled passion—some might say obsession—to succeed. When I was twenty-six I barely knew what I wanted for breakfast in the morning let alone what I wanted to do with my life.

[34] No one asked Clydie Clyde if he agreed or not.

the air; Beck's firing soon followed. The two stayed together, however, moving down market yet again and ending up at New Haven's KC101.[35] "Beck was no longer a boy wonder destined for greatness," Zaitchik writes. "He was staring failure in the face."

Not quite. In one of those odd little twists of fate that would change Beck's life forever, tiny little KC101 was sold to Clear Channel Communications. Clear Channel, though still small, was on its way to becoming much bigger—helped by the coming deregulation that allowed conglomerates to own many more stations than in years past. Clear Channel also picked up another station at the same time, WELI, New Haven's leading talk radio station. Having the two stations under the same umbrella—and finding himself suddenly part of an emerging media empire— would gain Beck his first real talk radio opportunities.

But first he had to finish going through the drugs, the booze, the blackouts, and the spiritual meltdown before rebuilding himself as the Glenn Beck we know today.

---

[35] Pat Gray is again with Beck, having joined Beck's show in 2009 after leaving Houston's conservative talk radio station, KSEV. Mike McGuff, on his blog site, calls Gray and Beck "BFFs." Makes them sound like a couple of cheerleader extras on *Glee.*

WEEK FIVE:
LISTING TO THE RIGHT

As month two begins, I'm on the shitlist.

In most cases a "shitlist" is purely metaphorical. When my wife is short a decent suit to wear for a client meeting because I forgot to pick up the dry cleaning, then I'm on the shitlist. When I fail to set the DVR to record *Nurse Jackie* because I'm too busy using the space for every NHL playoff game I can find, then I'm on the shitlist. And when I forget to give my oldest dog her incontinence pill and then let her spend the day curled up on the sofa, then I'm *really* on the shitlist.

In the Twittersphere lists are real; the idea is to group people who fall into a self-defined common category so that others can follow the entire group with one click. You can build and manage your own or let automated tools do the work for you. This simple yet brilliant device creates community, helps build followers, and encourages like-minded conversation, effectively expanding your Twitter experience in interesting and unpredictable ways.

Apparently somebody out there decided to set up a shitlist and I'm on it. Cool.

The creator and manager of the list calls himself @NoWingnuts and is an ultra-liberal tweeter living abroad who has apparently appointed himself the all-knowing arbiter of what is and is not worth tweeting about. His list gathers together several hundred people he feels are ultra-conservative wingnuts (hence the no-wing-nuts appellation), and then he's chosen to both "block" those people from following him and to send out the list to his followers so that they, too, can block the list members. He calls this the Shithead List.

Convoluted, and not without irony. I love irony.

First of all, liberals usually scream rather loudly about freedom of speech—think the ACLU[36]—and are generally stereotyped as openminded and inclusive, supposedly willing to engage in all types of conversation. @NoWingnuts, however, encourages people to block free speech; apparently he prefers to tweet back and forth only with people who already agree with him. Secondly, he's actually offering free publicity for those on the list. Our names—and the tweets that go with them—are enjoying the added circulation of his 600-plus followers. Thanks to his efforts I'm actually gaining liberal followers rather than finding myself blocked. And finally, there's the name calling. Shithead? Really? Is that necessary?

"Shitheads" isn't the best list I'm on. That honor belongs to one entitled *Malum-Nequam-Despictivus*, a list created by @LibforLife, a woman from this side of the Atlantic and every bit as liberal as @NoWingnuts. The Latin translates roughly as *Evil-Worthless-Despicable* which, I assume, is how @LibforLife regards the 169 members she's pigeonholed thusly. I do give her props for the Latin,

---

[36] The American Civil Liberties Union, or ACLU, too often gets a bad rap. As Michael Douglas' character, President Andrew Shephard, says in *The American President* to opponent Bob Rumson (played with fantastic oiliness by Richard Dreyfuss), "For the record: yes, I am a card-carrying member of the ACLU. But the more important question is why aren't you, Bob? Now, this is an organization whose sole purpose is to defend the Bill of Rights, so it naturally begs the question: Why would a senator, his party's most powerful spokesman and a candidate for President, choose to reject upholding the Constitution?" I find it disconcerting and hypocritical that the far right hates the ACLU given that the former argues for the same obsessive constitutional oversight as the latter.

though, since she has at least attempted some nomenclatural creative-ity as opposed to, say, Shitheads. But it's clear that conservatives do not hold the patent on extremism. Not at all.

@LibforLife describes herself as a Democratic Socialist, just the kind of person that many of the people I follow are most frightened by. Like @NoWingnuts, @LibforLife consistently demonstrates in-tolerance and frequently resorts to name-calling:

> LibforLife: This dumb f***er @FixtheLiberals following me thinks Glenn c**khole Beck is a LIBERAL!! Wow, a real live fascist.

Pause.

What?

I need to read that again.

> LibforLife: This dumb f***er @FixtheLiberals following me thinks Glenn c**khole Beck is a LIBERAL!! Wow, a real live fascist.

I've never run into @FixtheLiberals before. I don't follow this particular tweep nor does he or she follow me. And yet my ad-mittedly absurd concept seems either to have leaked out or has emerged entire in some strange Newton-and-Leibniz[37] way. Has someone else carried the Glenn-Beck-is-a-Liberal idea out into the Twittersphere? Could there really be two of us?

---

[37] Both Isaac Newton and Gottfried Wilhelm Leibniz developed what we now know as calculus within just a few years of each other. Neither knew of the other's work. A similar simultaneity is found between Charles Darwin and Alfred Russel Wallace with respect to natural selection.

Despite the singularity of the remark, I'm suddenly encouraged to step up my tweeting even more. What would thirty per day do? Or forty? Or fifty?

ᙣ ᙕ

I get up from the sofa where my wife and I had settled in to watch the morning's local news just a few minutes earlier. Erin Fehlau seems far too chipper for 5:30 in the morning, and I'm just not interested in high school lacrosse scores.

"Where are you going?" my wife asks.

"Upstairs."

She knows the code. I'm heading up to check my Twitter account. "Already?" she says. As I climb the steps, I hear her trailing argument. "I think this project is taking over your life." I stop three steps up and lean back over the railing. "Of course it's not," I tell her.

So what if my back is a bit sore from leaning over a keyboard for hours and hours every day? So what if 80 percent of our conversation now has to do with my follower count, the prevalence of Twitter spam, and why @Rachelmaddow hasn't yet caught wind of my brilliance? I'm still getting my regular work done, aren't I? I'm generating the invoices, managing our sales pipeline, and doing all those other little things that keep our business running. What's the big deal?

"You're not sleeping very well," she says. "And you're cranky." I ignore this last comment and restart my climb. When I get up to my office, I flip on the computer and wait impatiently for Microsoft's tedious and time-consuming boot.

It's true that I have a bit of a problem with obsession, though I'm no Adrian Monk. Most of the time it's pretty innocuous, more like intense serial activity rather than real compulsion. Still, it can get the better of me now and then.

Once, several years ago, I found myself without a book to read just before boarding a long flight. I popped into the airport bookstore to pick up something that would at least hold my attention until I fell asleep. Unfortunately, the airport was in Israel and most of the books were backward.

Of the small selection of books in English, few were recognizable and many were romances. One jumped out at me, however: *Seeing* by Jose Saramago, an author I'd never heard of but who had won the Nobel Prize for Literature[38] a few years back. The premise of the book—that people simply woke up one Election Day and decided, *en masse*, not to vote—intrigued me. I bought the book and devoured it during the long transatlantic flight.

As I turned the last page somewhere over Newfoundland it occurred to me that there were many works of great literature that I would never get around to reading, would perhaps never even know about. I decided that it might be fun to read a book by anyone who had ever won the Nobel Prize in Literature.

For those who have now pigeonholed me into the "wacko" category, know that you're not alone.

The project started out simply enough. The Nobel Prize website posts a complete list of all the winners and a quick scan revealed that I had already read roughly a quarter of the slightly more than 100 authors. Many came as high school assignments: Hemingway, Faulkner, T.S. Eliot, and William Golding, to name just a few. Roughly another quarter were authors I had heard of and had always planned to read but had never gotten around to, writers like Pablo

---

[38] Upon his death in 1895, Alfred Nobel willed the largest share of his fortune to a series of prizes in a variety of disciplines; these came to be known as the Nobel Prizes. The first given for Literature was awarded in 1901 to a French poet, Sully Prudhomme. Yeah, I'd never heard of him, either.

Neruda, Samuel Beckett, and Pearl S. Buck. My mission would give me the chance to fill these obvious gaps in my literary education.

I told my wife about the project and she thought it seemed interesting. "Good for you," she said. "You love to read and it's nice to have a goal. You just go on ahead."[39]

I was ready to dive in but first I needed rules. What good is a project without rules? I built a spreadsheet to keep track of everything and checked off all those authors whom I had already read: nothing like a few quick wins to build momentum. Then I drafted three simple guidelines. Number one: whenever possible, I would read a complete book. For the essayists, poets, and short story writers on the list that would mean finding a bound collection, not just trolling through old anthologies and picking out a sample here and there. Number two: once begun, a volume had to be finished. I couldn't begin something, decide that I didn't like it, toss it aside, and then pick up something else by the same author. And, finally, number three: I couldn't read anything else except Nobel Prize winners until I was done.[40] I also added two "recommendations" to my list, preferences, but not requirements. I wouldn't automatically select the shortest work by an author just to breeze through as quickly as I could, nor would I necessarily read an author's best-known work. For a playwright that might mean reading a book of essays instead, or, for a novelist, a rare foray into poetry.

I first scoured my own bookshelves for any qualifying volumes I owned but had never opened, a venture that yielded just a few. I

---

[39] She sometimes talks to me this way. I recognize the sarcasm and find it endearing. Basically her rule is that she doesn't get wound around the axle when I get an idea like this as long as it doesn't involve power tools.

[40] Yes, this is me. Can't help it. This is only one example of my obsessive inclinations, and not the most ridiculous by far. That would be the time I set up a Microsoft Project plan to manage my wedding. Turns out the critical path was getting the rings on time.

pulled them from their snug slots and placed them bedside in a small pile. I then headed to the library with the full winners' list in hand, nicely sorted and alphabetized. Deciding to start with some of the more contemporary authors, names like Seamus Heaney or J.M. Coetzee, I checked the library computer and effortlessly tracked them down.

I'm a voracious and rapid reader; I knocked a few more authors off the list pretty quickly and I was enjoying the discovery of new voices and new ideas. Orhan Pamuk's *My Name is Red* enthralled me, as did Doris Lessing's *The Cleft*. Saul Bellow and Isaac Bashevis Singer I cared for less than I expected to, Alexander Solzhenitsyn and Derek Walcott more.

I quickly discovered the limitations of a small-town library. Beyond the current and popular authors (those I had found, along with others like Toni Morrison and Harold Pinter, both previously read), the library held books by only the most famous names, John Steinbeck, for example, and Hermann Hesse. Among the one hundred-plus Nobel winners there were many far too obscure for a local library.

My next stop was Barnes and Noble, a place I frequented often over the next several months. Here I made significant progress, often picking up eight or ten books at a time.[41] I slogged through Gunter Grass and Thomas Mann, then breezed through Dario Fo and Nadine Gordimer. I read poetry by Boris Pasternak, Jean-Paul Sartre's *No Exit*, and Bertrand Russell's *Why I Am Not A Christian*. As each title fell I went back to my list and struck through the author's name, pleased to see my continued progress with each thin line.

---

[41] For those wondering why I didn't just hit Amazon.com, it's because I wanted to see and feel the books, to sample a few pages randomly here and there in order to pick one that I thought I'd be likely to enjoy. Amazon did come in quite handy later on as the names on the list reached further into obscurity and even B&N couldn't justify using up the shelf space.

Then it got tough. Trust me: there are names on that list that I'm pretty sure most literature professors have never heard of. One by one I tracked them down, read them, ticked them off. Nelly Sachs, Frederic Mistral, Selma Lagerlöf, and Bjornstjerne Bjornson. Romain Rolland, Harry Martinson, Jacinto Benavente, and Maurice Maeterlinck.[42] Finally, it all came down to Pontoppidan.

Henrik Pontoppidan won the Nobel Prize for Literature in 1917[43] for his "authentic descriptions of present-day life in Denmark" and will forever serve as a personal symbol of both obsession and determination. Pontoppidan, author of more than forty books, was sixty years old at the time of his award. Only five had ever been translated into English, and I couldn't find any of them anywhere. I trolled used bookstores, both physically and virtually. Two dusty, out-of-the-way collector sites in Manchester, New Hampshire yielded nothing, nor did an exhaustive review of Abebooks, a premier on-line site for aficionados of the rare and unusual. I checked academic sites and library sites hoping that somewhere an internet interconnection would prove helpful. I posted on blogs and chat sites, made phone calls, even enlisted friends to help me. This was the very last author, and I would not be beaten.

I had absolutely nothing riding on the outcome. No monetary wager that I would finish the list, no promise to anyone, no ego involved except my own. Yet I had to find a book by Pontoppidan. At one point I thought I had located something at a print-on-demand

---

[42] For those curious, France boasts the greatest number of prize winners, followed by the United States, United Kingdom, and Germany. Jose Saramago is the only winner from Portugal. Other soloists include Belgium, India, and Israel.

[43] He actually shared the prize, something not uncommon prior to 1920 but rare afterwards. The co-winner was Karl Adolph Gjellerup. The book I read of his was *The Pilgrim Kamanita: A Legendary Romance*. It was god-awful.

site[44] only to discover that when the book arrived, despite the publisher's claim, it was not an English translation.

Eventually one of those friends, a co-worker with equally fanatical tendencies, came across something promising. Back in 2006 Microsoft had decided to digitize a very large collection of old books from the University of California and had made them available online.[45] Dedicated digging finally unearthed Pontoppidan's *Emanuel (or Children of the Soil)* in an English translation from 1896. One rapid (and free) download later my screen filled with an amateurish line drawing of the original cover, faded yellow, with Pontoppidan's name center stage. Rarely have I been so happy.

But somehow digital bits just didn't feel right to me. I'm old school; I needed a book, something I could hold in my hands, an object with pages I could turn and a spine I could crack.[46]

A book I would have. I saved the downloaded file to a flash drive and later that day drove to Staples with a very clear image of what I wanted: a printed, double-sided hard copy (including the cover, in color), trimmed to the appropriate trade paperback dimensions and bound in a plastic cover. Once completed, I used a label maker and

---

[44] Since so much literature has been digitized there are now publishers who create a book only when it's ordered. The results are reasonably professional if somewhat generic. I acquired several books this way. My favorite is *The Charles Men* by von Heidenstam, who won the Nobel in 1916. The book inexplicably has a photograph of a green bicycle leaning against a doorway gracing the cover. There are no bicycles anywhere in the book.

[45] The project, Live Search Books, was abandoned in 2008 but managed to complete the digitization of about 750,000 books and over 80 million journal articles. These digitized versions are now available through the Internet Archive.

[46] Though I sometimes read a book on my iPad, I've never grown fond of digital readers. I like books with margins I can write in, sitting on bookshelves that surround a fireplace and a couple of comfortable chairs. It's how I want to spend my last days, surrounded by these old friends and having—as a classic *Twilight Zone* episode put it—"time enough at last."

crafted a spine with the author's name prominently displayed and carefully affixed, using a ruler to make sure it was centered both vertically and horizontally.

Emanuel existed. Though he cost me nearly forty bucks I have never felt so stupidly self-satisfied. I took it home and read it; it was okay.

My wife has grown quite used to my obsessions, and I imagine she was waiting for the next one now that I was done chasing Alfred. She's more than aware of how my habits shift when I'm in one of these states. I plan my days accordingly and shuffle priorities to suit my mood, sometimes haphazardly. So when she tells me that this current project, this Twittering and scribbling, has an *Invasion of the Body Snatchers* feel to it, I should probably listen to her.

When I'm living between obsessions, I generally segment my days into discrete pieces, marking each task as complete before moving on to the next. I actually make lists.[47] Most of the items are simple— things like balancing the bank accounts or checking the dogs for ticks—and I usually get them done by eight or nine in the morning. This gives me a necessary but artificial feeling of accomplishment and usually carries me through an hour or two of what my wife calls "counting loose change," her interesting euphemism for procrastination. Loose change can be anything from checking the NASDAQ to watching a couple of YouTube videos to looking up old school friends on Facebook and misremembering how close we all were.

Eventually the warmth of accomplishment wears off along with the morning's coffee buzz, and I realize I have to get something done. So I try to write for a couple of hours. Only I realize that

---

[47] I know that lots of people make lists, but nobody that I know of but me puts "make list" on the top of the list just so I can cross it off and feel a small sense of accomplishment.

before I write I should check the @BeckIsALib account to see how I'm doing. Do I have more followers this morning? Yes, a couple. More mentions? Yes, quite a few, thank you. Feeling pretty good at this point, I decide to check my Klout. Perhaps it's gone up since last night when I checked it before going to bed, or yesterday before dinner, or yesterday afternoon (twice).

And since I'm on Twitter anyway, maybe I'll just read a few recent tweets. I glance at one or two, and by the time I've finished another thirteen have arrived. A couple of those are related to the ones I've just read, so naturally I have to read those, too.

One tweet rubs me the wrong way; I decide to respond. No harm in that. I look at the clock in the lower corner of my monitor and see that it's only half-past nine. I do have a few more things to get done this morning, but there's plenty of time. I'll just finish this tweet quickly and then perhaps check the market open. Earlier this morning the futures were up and if it carries over into the first few minutes of trading I may want to update my investments spreadsheet to reflect the market's optimistic outlook.

Back to the Twitter feed: I see a response to my response, check it, and find out that I've been called a name, though not a terribly hateful one. Still, I don't like rudeness when I'm trying to have a polite conversation. I respond to the response to the response, remaining on the high road, until I finally get a grudging apology, though still with a backhanded attack on my position.

The timeline cascade quickens as more people come on line. Several more interesting tweets have added themselves to the queue; one of them is about Glenn Beck so I have to respond. I haven't forgotten my main message and I take any opportunity I find to reinforce the fact that I think Beck is a liberal actor playing the part of a conservative nutcase. My interjection births an exchange with @CalLiberal14, a leftist from the west coast, and @Truthupholder, a likeminded tweep who shares the same opinions:

CalLiberal14: I am literally scared to death of the right wing fake Christians that are followers of Glenn Beck. Are they brainwashed or just plain nuts?

Truthupholder: @CalLiberal14 Wow... It's a very thin line between brainwashed and nuts. Glenn Beck followers are creepy.

BeckIsALib: @Truthupholder @CalLiberal14 To me Beck is just an entertainer (and a smart businessman). He actually has liberal in his background, if you can believe it.

Truthupholder: @BeckIsALib @CalLiberal14 I would laugh at Beck as a clown... if there were not so many that take him seriously... He sets a dangerous standard.

BeckIsALib: @Truthupholder @CalLiberal14 Ahh, but the more of us who laugh—loudly and publicly—the less dangerous he becomes. Beck harms true conservatism.

Truthupholder: @BeckIsALib @CalLiberal14 On this we both AGREE!!! We must all laugh and laugh loudly :) Thanks for the reminder not to take clowns too seriously.

I look again at the clock on my monitor: it's nearing noon. I don't quite know where the morning went, but I'm hungry and my checklist remains largely unscathed. Perhaps my wife is right.

ಜ ೞ

Week Five has unquestionably turned out to be the most interesting week since I began this exercise. Apart from the whole "shitlist" thing and the descent into Latin-tinged Twitterhell, I've made it onto another half-dozen lists. All of them, not surprisingly, list to the right. One of them is administered by the aforementioned @RonWitherspoon; according to Klout he is one of the top few "Taste Makers" on conservatism in politics, and he apparently likes me even though we only sometimes agree. He has #FF'd me a few times, and has given me a friendly warning about a troll that he suspects might be trailing me.[48]

Ron's list is a collection of several hundred Klout-heavy individuals. Several, like @MichiganLakes, have over 50,000 tweets and thousands of followers. Many of them are what Klout calls "Thought Leaders." (I am a mere "Explorer," which makes me the Twitterverse equivalent of the kid on the playground standing fourth in line for the seesaw.)

I think my favorite list has to be "Good People 2." The list creator, a conservative pro-Israel blogger named @Ayalon, has an incredible reach in Twitter, and he effectively engages people on both sides of the spectrum in rational and often wise discourse. Like me, he is not overly fond of the extremists and, also like me, has occasionally been mistaken for a liberal, mostly because he doesn't treat social issues as if everyone to the left of Pat Robertson is morally leprotic.

The second reason I like the list is simply because of the name: "Good People 2." That means @Ayalon has a "Good People 1" list somewhere but it grew so large that he needed another list. I like

---

[48] I was fuzzy on the whole "troll" thing for a while. At first I thought it was just anybody with a tendency to be a pain in the ass. Then I thought that maybe it was a code for lurkers, people who hang about in the dark shadows, like trolls under a bridge. But then I realized there was already a word for the lurkers: it's "lurkers." It turns out that a Twitterverse troll is a truly nasty piece of work, a person who posts with the sole purpose of creating maximum disruption and argument. Trolls don't really care what the conversation is about; they just want to hear the noise. I once had an uncle who behaved that way at Passover dinners.

that he thinks there are so many good people in the Twitterverse, and that I'm one of them.

My name also shows up on a few esoteric lists, collections of tweeps that are somehow connected in the deep recesses of one person's mind but which otherwise appear patternless. One of those, simply entitled "People," is run by a woman from Nevada called, equally simply, @NVWoman. Her list seems randomly populated by people she finds interesting, sometimes leading to jolting disconnects from one tweet to another:

> NVWoman: RT @Beenthereandback Right now Bernanke is juicing the stock market to try and create more jobs. Really running monetary and fiscal policy.

> NVWoman: RT @Cranley4898: @Recon4 @TakeitBack "How low can you stoop!" Voyeuristic death movie freak and #EDL hag.

This last comment, at first very confusing, appears to be aimed at defending the #EDL tag, though I'm not exactly sure what that defense is supposed to be.[49]

The phenomenon of lists reinforces an apparently nascent human need to categorize. I remember that as a child I spent hours and hours with an ever-increasing collection of baseball cards, organizing and re-organizing them, first by team, then by position or batting average or runs batted in.

---

[49] The #EDL tag means either "English Defence League" or "Ewok Defence League." The former is a far-right protest movement birthed in anti-Islamist sentiment while the latter is a counter-effort to hijack the hash tag in order to render it meaningless in the Twittersphere. One explanation, found on a comment site, explains: "Bring down the racist EDL scum on Twitter by posting racist comments about the immigrant Stormtrooper population, coming over to Endor, building their Deathstars. Mark everything with the #EDL tag, and hope that the real racists [sic] tw*ts go away." And there you have it: the Twitterverse equivalent of a border war.

Sometimes I'd separate out those I expected to see in the Hall of Fame one day, wrapping each in plastic on the off chance that the cards might someday be worth something.[50]

We love lists. *The Book of Lists*, originally published in 1977, rose up the ranks of bestseller lists and spawned several sequels. Today we have ESPN's daily "Top 10 Plays," along with numerous shows about the top rock songs, the top sexiest bodies, and the top vacation spots. Even CNBC has gotten into the act with its annual list of top states for business.[51] We must have a gene for it somewhere. I suppose we all want to be on a list of some kind, even one as generically titled as @NVWoman's "People."

Given that I've become even more concerned with my follower count, I'm hoping that the lists I'm on will connect me with an expanded set of tweeps. Lately I've become somewhat isolated, conversing repeatedly with the same people over and over again, locked in the Twittersphere's equivalent of a traffic roundabout. In Kloutian terms, I haven't done much to expand my "amplification." I'm hoping that the new lists will provide me with both interesting people to follow and interesting people who might want to follow me.

I've also started losing a few followers here and there. It was a shock to wake up the other morning and find that my follower count had dropped from 156 to 153, and that's after I had already winnowed out the spammers and marketers. I know I shouldn't feel the subtle stings of rejection but I do.

Everything I've read about Twitterverse culture told me to expect that this would happen, that certain followers would sample my

---

[50] Like most, my collection ended up in the trash which, ironically, is why those forty-year-old cards *are* worth something—for someone. Ditto for comic books and first girlfriends.

[51] Currently Virginia, displacing last year's winner, Colorado, which slipped to fifth. Alaska ranked forty-ninth, up from dead last the year before. Palinites, take note.

tweets like hors d'oeuvres at a sales conference meet-and-greet and then, after a few tastes, decide that I wasn't interesting, or that I was annoying, or that I simply didn't agree with them and so wasn't worth their time.

The first reason—that I'm not interesting—just isn't possible; I'm incredibly interesting, with cogent, intelligent, and witty-slash-pithy sayings mashed carefully into a 140-character container. So that can't be it.

Annoying? Possibly. I've been told that once or twice, particularly when I pedantically correct another's obscure historical or literary reference, for example. My wife occasionally teases me about it, threatening to buy me a t-shirt with a bright red "P"[52] on the front, and a cape to go with it.

I think the third option is the most likely, though: I don't believe the same things they do. If there's one thing I've noticed throughout the Twitterverse, it's the propensity for people to want to converse exclusively with those who agree with them. So you get mundane dialogues like this, written in treacly, aren't-we-so-clever tones of voice:

IrisGrower: Rasmussen: By 81-11, adults say the right of free speech is more important than making sure no one is offended by what others say.

MrsMiniver: @IrisGrower: The other 11% must work in government and media.

IrisGrower: @MrsMiniver: And in our schools. The educational establishment is arguably the most politically correct of all.

---

[52] For "Pedanticman!"

IrisGrower: Indeed, don't know how I missed them! Maybe I was lumping them in with government workers. I'll tell myself that anyway. :)

This conversation isn't in any way interesting or profound. People want free speech. Other people are too thin-skinned. The problem is with government and education.

Cue the Seinfeldian *yaddas*.

Maybe I'm asking too much; given the gazillions of tweets each day you have to expect that the bulk of them tend toward meaninglessness and inanity. Still, I prefer the interesting back-and-forth emerging from two intelligent people in polite disagreement, to the mutual admiration that comes from people giddily clacking away with someone whose opinions they already share. It's like watching two adolescents whispering in each other's ears while a third, just off to one side, grows a worrisome frown. In the Twitterverse I've found more of the former than I expected and more of the latter than I wanted. It's why I often jump midstream into someone else's conversation. I just want to see what happens when disagreements arise.

Or perhaps I have a bit of troll in me.

Michael Charney

WEEK SIX:
TWITTERDREAMS

H ere's how I'm changing:
    A typical day would normally begin around dawn when
one of my two dogs—usually the older one—awakens
asking to go out. I escort them downstairs and set them loose inside
our large fenced-in backyard, then step into the kitchen to flip on the
coffee. Sometimes I'll check the temperature in the house and turn
up the heat a couple of degrees; New England mornings are chilly
more often than not and my wife, currently carrying around her own
personal summer, likes it cooler at night than I do.

Once the coffeemaker beeps and the dogs, now back inside, dig
into their breakfast, I pour my first cup of coffee, add sugar, and then
settle in to read for a bit, sometimes the previous day's Wall Street
Journal or the neighborhood paper, sometimes a book. After that
comes thirty minutes or so on the elliptical machine, and then more
coffee and a bit of revolving television.

The television routine is nearly always the same (much as the
overall routine is nearly always the same). The Weather Channel is
invariably first because simply looking outside isn't good enough for
anyone anymore. I need to know how to plan my day, and that
involves avoiding anything that might be wet, or blowing on me, or

beating on me.[53] After the weather I spend some time with Becky Quick and her *Squawk Box* companions over on CNBC. I like to know where the markets are headed and whether I'm likely to be in a good mood or a bad mood by 4:00 p.m. Eastern. Then I flip over to *SportsCenter* to catch a few of the previous day's highlights because I'm a man and that's the rule.

Only not today, not after more than a month immersed in the political Twittermind. Today I watched *Fox and Friends*. I have never, ever watched it before. I have never even felt the temptation to watch it before. Yet today, inexplicably, I did.

I didn't tune in for research or to see whether the network was truly "fair and balanced," nor did I watch it because it just happened to be the channel left on last night before we went up to bed. I watched it because I wanted to.

Turns out it's not that great. It doesn't stack up particularly well when compared to, say, *Good Morning America* or *Today*. The lighting is rude, the makeup caked, the set spartan. The hosts—Gretchen, Steve, and Brian—are all quite likeable but could look a bit better if the show spent a few more bucks on the basics. There was also a "Guest Legal Analyst" on this morning, Peter Johnson, Jr., who argued the issues much like I did when I wrote that paper for Mr. Winston in the eleventh grade. The guy is really pasty looking, too. All in all the show looked to me a tad shoddy. The graphics are nice, though.

I sat through three entire stories before I got angry.

The first had to do with a recent incident involving the arrival and departure protocols for planes carrying the First Lady. During a recent trip from somewhere to somewhere else, Michelle Obama's plane was forced to abort a landing at Andrews Air Force Base

---

[53] That last one refers to the sun, not some surly neighbor or an overly aggressive clerk at Target.

because it came too close to a C-17 military transport. Fox's talking heads were once again up in arms about air traffic controllers and the potentially lethal mistakes they sometimes make.[54] The hosts bantered a bit about it as morning show hosts often do, but the story was without any particular point of view. There was nothing about special treatment for Michelle, nothing snarky about how the new protocols might screw it up for us ordinary people.[55]

The second story introduced the audience to a brewing skirmish between Donald Trump and Jerry Seinfeld. The battle erupted when Jerry backed out of a commitment to attend a fundraiser for St. Jude's Children's Hospital sponsored by the Eric Trump Foundation. Eric is Don's son. Jerry changed his mind after becoming increasingly uncomfortable with some of the more absurd political Trump-rants that Donald, in his quest for attention and a possible 2012 presidential run, had decided were of supreme importance to all America. It wasn't the economy or the housing market or the Middle East, however. It was instead the all-encompassing subject of the current president's birthplace.[56] Jerry decided that he wanted to distance himself from that sort of craziness and so begged off the appearance. Trump then fired off a nasty letter disparaging Seinfeld's anemic show, *The Marriage Ref*, remarking how he, Trump, kept his, Trump's, commitment to show up, but that apparently Jerry didn't even have sense enough to feel shame for breaking his promise to all

---

[54] Right around this time there were a couple of incidents where air traffic controllers had actually fallen asleep on the job. C'mon, people: radar screens may look like an Atari video game, but they're not, okay?

[55] The fact that I even noticed the absence of such snarkiness tells more about my own prejudice than about Fox News which, in this case, was neither fair nor unfair, balanced nor unbalanced, just dull.

[56] Trump is currently using every opportunity to make a fool of himself, as if *Celebrity Apprentice* didn't already provide him ample opportunity. Hell, even Michele Bachmann told him to give it a rest.

those kids. *Fox and Friends* boldly displayed the text of Don's letter next to a smiling photo of Jerry. The photo chose not to respond.

By now I'm thinking that this show isn't half-bad, despite the poorly made-up faces and the biased legal analyst. Maybe a bit more Toledo Mud Hens than Boston Red Sox, but still a refreshing break from the more polished smiles of its elder brethren.

After a brief commercial encouraging me to buy gold, story number three came on, the one that made me angry. As it turns out, I don't get angry at Fox—quite the opposite. Fox is actually broadcasting a story worth hearing but which I haven't seen elsewhere: the ignominy of the EPA Rap.

That's right: our tax dollars are being used by the Environmental Protection Agency to create and broadcast a rap song designed to encourage energy savings as a way to combat global warming. The song, entitled "Click It—Flip It," suffers from some seriously awful lyrics:

> *The climate is changing and that's a fact,*
> *Bears don't know when to take a nap,*
> *On top of that it won't be cool*
> *When the flood waters rise and mosquitoes rule.*
> *It's time to get off the couch and start to move.*
> *Come on and click it, flip it, turn the handle to the right,*
> *Turn off the water, twist the handle real tight.*
> *Slip on your sneakers, lace 'em up tight,*
> *Leave the car parked, you know that's all right.*

Let's not even talk about whether we should be spending money on this, whether the rap's target audience cares a whit about the issue in question, or whether the drugs the songwriters were obviously taking at the time were any good at all. Let's not even debate global warming's existence and whether, if it does exist, it's man's fault, and whether, if it is man's fault we can even do anything about it at this point. Let's just focus on one basic thing: this song sucks.[57]

Public money pays for this campaign. You and I fund the EPA, and whether or not you agree with the EPA's mission, this particular program has exactly zero chance of meeting any of its rather spurious goals. While such a ridiculous campaign would seem a waste of money at any time, in this particular economic climate (with unemployment exceeding nine percent and government coffers painfully shallow), it makes no sense at all.

Hence my anger and my grudging appreciation for Fox's decision to run the story. The part that scares me most, though, isn't my irritated response; it's that I think (though I can't be sure) that a couple of months ago I might have felt differently. Have I begun to ride that mental sled downhill? Am I believing things that I wouldn't have in the past simply because I've been thinking about them more?

α ∝

With the curtain rising on Week Six, my stats look pretty good. I have 223 followers and sit on eleven lists. I receive regular mentions and each day a few more of my tweets are retweeted by others. My all-important Klout stands at forty-eight and my comparable Twitalyzer ranking puts me in the top 20 percent of all influencers in the Twittersphere. Perhaps most interesting are the three independent references I've seen suggesting that Glenn Beck just might be other than he appears. I'm feeling a bit proud, as if I've actually accomplished something.

---

[57] Before you come to the conclusion that I'm just an old white guy who only listens to Jim Croce and Joni Mitchell, let me tell you that I like rap and hip-hop and both have a place in my rather extensive music collection. I've also spent time in a mosh pit at a Marilyn Manson concert. I'm quite open-minded about music, but if the lyrics don't scan, they don't scan. End of story.

Most of my forty or fifty daily tweets remain largely generic, though I'm dropping in thoughts about Beck at least a few times a day. If, however, I see someone who is consistently pro-Beck, then I'll launch a tweet or two toward that person in the hopes of engaging in a targeted conversation. That's what I did with one very vocal young man who is about as pro-Beck as anyone I've seen: @ReaganStyle.

Victor Mooney, aka @ReaganStyle,[58] an ambitious teenager from Long Island, New York who first joined Twitter in September 2009, was formerly an ardent supporter of Barack Obama. His Twitter bio tells us that he was "turned Constitutionalist by @GlennBeck." He has been on Beck's radio program—you can see a YouTube video of the interview uploaded from *The Daily Beck*—and is one of only twenty-five people that Glenn Beck follows on Twitter. That puts Victor in some very lofty company; Beck also follows Karl Rove, Jack Welch, Penn Jillette, and The Onion.

Victor, a Klout-designated "Thought Leader" with an overall score of sixty-four, has thousands of retweets, graces hundreds of lists, and has more than 4,000 followers. Twitalyzer has him in the top seven percent of all Twitter influencers. He also administers and writes for a blog, *Truth for American Teens*, where he argues intelligently and respectfully on a variety of issues, from the U.S. Constitution to the tragic shooting of Representative Gabrielle Giffords. I decided to follow Victor early on partly because he's a major name in my corner of the Twittersphere but also because he's a convert. Converts are often the most fervent in their beliefs,[59] and I thought that if I could get him to admit that I might have a point about Beck,

---

[58] @ReaganStyle is a public figure, having appeared on the Glenn Beck radio show. I've taken the liberty of using his real names, both human and @.

[59] Just ask an ex-smoker, or anyone who has ever had one for a sister.

maybe the idea would have some legs. Maybe Victor himself would pass the idea along.

Victor doesn't follow me, but since I follow him I can easily engage in conversation by simply replying to his tweets and seeing what happens, or by @naming him in my tweets and asking him questions directly. Most of his tweets (like most everyone's tweets) are pretty generic (though political), but sometimes he specifically brings up Glenn Beck; when he does I take the opening given, as in this brief excerpt of a recent back-and-forth, which followed an announcement that Beck was returning to the air after some time off:

> ReaganStyle: @GlennBeck is back from his break........so refreshing...

> BeckIsALib: @ReaganStyle I know you're a fan--saw your video-- but Beck is an actor. He used to be liberal, and will go wherever the dollars are. He hurts us.

> ReaganStyle: @BeckIsALib Sure he is. I know what I believe and I'm pretty sure I know where GB stands on the issues. But thanks anyway.

Though the exchange is brief, it still surprises me. Victor defies every stereotype I've ever held about how a typical Beckian is expected to behave: he is polite. Even when faced with an idea that is completely counter to what he believes to be true, he remains civil and kind. He talks to me. He even throws me a little bone with the "sure he is" in response to my insistence that Beck is an actor. Victor just thinks that Beck uses his acting skills in support of a conservative mission. He makes his points and offers his opinions with model civility, behavior seemingly absent from much of today's political positioning. Contrast Victor's respectful demeanor to those of several leftists who regularly belittle Beck:

> Threepics: Take it as an honor that a twisted demented f**k like Glenn Beck and his pathetic followers hate you.

> MovieLover: Glenn Beck is a blubbering vagina of hate, intolerance, and misinformation. He makes other Republicans look sane. A daunting task indeed.

Whether you agree or disagree with the sentiments offered, I doubt you would argue that either of the above tweets are at all genteel. Perhaps those on the left can defend various meanings for the word "is," but "blubbering vagina of hate" allows for no alternative interpretation.

Not all those with similar opinions sound like these, but it is much, much easier to find the left ranting about Beck than the right ranting about the left ranting about Beck. I find myself wondering how much the media—with their rampant repetition of hate signs and foul mouths—color my expectations. Certainly what I found (generalized though it is) has proven other than I anticipated. When I separate content from tone, it's clear to me that the right is simply nicer than the left. The left is where I found nearly all of the foul language and most of the name-calling, where dismissive attitudes were punctuated with just-plain-rudeness. Many sounded like Little League parents who were really, really pissed off at the umpire and had decided to throw beer bottles on the field while their kids stared on in disbelief.

Such behavior exists on the right, but having now read thousands and thousands of tweets over the past four weeks—and most of them from the right—I've found that the ratio is completely inverted from what I had primed myself for. I had clearly stepped into the quicksand of stereotype.

So where did my stereotypes arise from? Why did I come into this exercise pre-supposing the opposite of what I found? Like just about everyone I knew growing up, I was raised by good, solid, middle-class Democrats. My stepfather worked for the U.S. Postal Service (for a while in the union, but later in management), and my mother typed letters and made appointments for salesmen at the Wm. Wrigley, Jr. Company's regional office. The first meant that weekends were odd, since my stepfather had a revolving work schedule that included every Sunday off along with one other rotating weekday, and the second meant that we had a lot of gum and candy in the house, all of it free. My dentist, Dr. Welcome[60] W. Adamson, was none too pleased. I loved it.

My first political memory rose from the black-and-white graininess emanating from a nineteen-inch Zenith on November 25, 1963, the first ever broadcast of a president's funeral. It was a Monday morning. My stepfather's introduction to my mother was still three years off, and she, post-divorce, had moved in with my grandparents out of necessity.

On the morning of the funeral, I remember lying on the carpet in front of the television with my legs waving behind me and my chin cupped in my hands. The rough carpet chafed both elbows. Through the living room window I could see a half-masted flag. I was five years old and mostly frustrated because the funeral was on every channel;[61] daytime shows I had come to count on for amusement, like Sheriff John and Captain Kangaroo, were nowhere to be found.

---

[60] Great name, isn't it? It's real, too. Almost (but not quite) makes you want to visit the dentist.

[61] We only had eight channels back then—2, 4, 5, 7, 9, 11, 13, and 28—and the last of these occupied a wavelength up in the UHF range where no amount of rabbit-ear

Words like "Camelot" and "widow" meant nothing to me; I'm not even sure why I was home on that weekday morning unless, perhaps, school had closed because of the tragedy. My mother was at work; my grandparents kept watch over me and my sister.

My mother had voted for Kennedy, as had her parents, both working class Jews who had migrated west from the Bronx. My grandparents had lived their entire lives in rented apartments, had stretched a pound of hamburger to feed five, and had never owned more than one car. My mother, to this day, doesn't know why she was a Democrat; she just was. When Lyndon Johnson ran for re-election in 1964 she never gave her allegiance a second's thought. (In talking to her recently I discovered that she barely remembered Barry Goldwater's name.) When 1968 came around she robotically punched her ballot for Hubert Humphrey, Alan Cranston, and Al Bellard. But there were too many people tired of LBJ's war and they believed that hope could only come with change; the majority populations in thirty-two of the fifty states disagreed with my mother, and Nixon eked into the White House.[62]

Nixon changed everything. While the highlights of his legacy have shifted in the years since his tenure ended in disgrace, he continues as a much-discussed figure. (There's no one I know who won't argue, however, that Nixon buried Camelot along with our idealized fantasies of the Presidency.) A recent Twitter exchange shows how conflicted people still are about him. The discussion began with the predictable shot at President Obama and his inadequacies, but the conversation quickly shifted, focusing instead on a president first elected nearly forty-five years ago.

---

twisting could bring in a decent signal. Yes, this was the dark ages. Our phones had cords, too, if you can believe that, and rotary dials.

[62] Nixon still had a Democratic Congress to deal with, though the GOP gained in both chambers, with a plus-five in the Senate and a plus-four in the House. Republicans also picked up five governorships in that election cycle.

Dandlittle: The more you see of President Obama and his thugs the more Nixon looks good.

Phillyfilly: @Dandlittle I admit that Nixon screwed up big time, but in many ways he was a great president. Obama doesn't come close.

BeckIsALib: @Phillyfilly @Dandlittle He was a terrible president who did some great things. But you can trace our national disdain for politics to him.

Phillyfilly: @BeckIsALib @Dandlittle He was a great president who did some terrible things. But you're right. His effect on politics is palpable.

Dandlittle: I can't agree. Nixon was a big government guy.

Phillyfilly: @BeckIsALib I don't agree with single issue focusing. Nixon was a genius at RealPolitik when that is what we needed.

BeckIsALib: @Phillyfilly @Dandlittle Hence my comment about some "great things." He also froze prices and wages in ways that no GOPer should ever consider.

Phillyfilly: @BeckIsALib @Dandlittle I agree with you about Nixon freezing wages and prices as a bad thing. He was horrible, and he was great.

The continued fascination with Nixon and his impact on how we feel about politics and politicians continues unabated. Whether you believe he was a great president who did some terrible things or a terrible president who did some great things doesn't even matter. What matters is the dialogue. Nixon is this nation's watershed president.

I remember exactly where I was the moment Nixon resigned in the same way that people know where they were when Neil Armstrong stepped onto the moon, when the Challenger exploded, or when the planes hit the Twin Towers. Each remains indelibly stamped in our collective yet still individual consciousness.

Watergate was everywhere (the overuse of the *dash*Gate appellation still years away), and children much younger than I bore strong opinions about Nixon and the entire Republican White House. Just barely sixteen, I believed that I was old enough to understand what was going on.

On the evening of August 8, 1974 I stood outside the main lodge of Camp JCA in the Malibu mountains where 150 kids ranging in age from six to thirteen spent two dry-as-a-bone weeks singing songs, creating crafts, hiking trails, and riding horses. It was my first year as a junior counselor, and gathered around me were the dozen or so eight- and nine-year-olds then in my charge. It was just after dinner and rather than everyone heading back to their cabins as they normally would before the evening's activities, everyone instead stood around outside the camp's dining hall; we all knew that Nixon was about to speak and we all expected him to resign.

The camp director had moved the camp's microphone in front of a tabletop radio that on most occasions pumped out classical music as background for the office secretary. When the broadcast began, the director flipped the switch that would air the news through a pair of blaring, pole-sitting speakers that looked just like the ones on those old M*A*S*H episodes. People stood still, staring up at those megaphone-shaped speakers as if waiting for orders from a commanding officer.

For the first few minutes of the speech Nixon circled around his eventful words, referring to "the long and difficult period of Watergate" and his history of having "never been a quitter." Most of the message washed over the kids. Some of the youngest grew a little restless. Then came the fateful statement: "Therefore, I shall resign the Presidency effective at noon tomorrow."

Deafening cheers broke out. Those who could erupted into two-fingered whistles; most just clapped, stamped their feet, or shouted their hurrahs. Without exception—right down to the six-year-olds in the youngest cabin, the six-year-olds who still occasionally wet their beds, who sometimes cried from homesickness, who ran frightened from yellow-jackets—every single person was ecstatic at the downfall of the president.

After that, the political world was never the same again. Anybody could have beaten Gerald Ford, and Jimmy Carter did. That election was my first opportunity to vote for president, and I dutifully followed the Democratic path laid out before me. Just like my mother in all the years before, I never gave it a second thought. But Carter's ineptness was obvious even to a kid like me on the back end of his teens. My first credit card[63] had a double-digit interest rate, the price of gas seemed outrageous and was still heading northward,[64] and my parents complained daily about the cost of milk, frozen vegetables, and just about everything else at Ralphs, our nearby supermarket.

---

[63] Issued to me by Bank of America when I was only sixteen. I had a $400 credit limit (nearly $2,000 today), which I rapidly tapped out. What were they thinking?

[64] In 1979, at the height of the campaign, a gallon of gas cost 86 cents. Doesn't sound like much until you adjust for inflation; in today's terms that would be $2.74 per gallon. But today that gallon would take you twenty-seven miles, while back then you could only go seventeen, so in relative dollars it would cost you about $4.25 to drive as far then as you can on a gallon today. Times were tough under Carter.

On foreign policy Carter showed early promise with his work mediating the Egyptian-Israeli peace accords, but the Iran hostage crisis pretty much wiped much of that legacy out of the public mind. By the time Reagan had finished stump-speeching his way across the country, the majority of people believed Carter the most inept president since Millard Fillmore.

When 1980 came along, I was disillusioned and ripe for a change. Carter had become a joke and Reagan was rallying conservatives in a disingenuous attempt to curry favor and motivate a previously unmotivated demographic. I migrated toward John Anderson, an Illinois congressman and moderate Republican, who, after losing the primaries to Reagan decided to run as an Independent.

Originally very conservative,[65] Anderson, once in Congress, saw his social policies shift leftward while his fiscal policies remained firmly on the right. Anderson was an attractive mix to a U.C. Berkeley graduate who had grown up in a Democratic household but had grown wary of the Democratic platform and was forced to watch while the extreme wing of the Republican Party began the slow but deliberate hijacking of the Republican *raison d'etre*.

Carter's lousy performance as Leader of the Free World pretty much guaranteed that he would join Herbert Hoover as the only modern-day, single-election president. Reagan swept him away—Anderson never had a chance[66]—and in the process changed the

---

[65] Anderson once introduced a constitutional amendment attempting to recognize Jesus Christ as the ultimate "law and authority" of the land. I imagine there are people today who would love to do the same, despite the whole church-and-state thing. Little known fact: in the last sixty years or so there have been more than fifty proposals for such an amendment.

[66] Anderson managed only 6.6 percent of the vote (and none of the Electoral College votes). It was no surprise since our system isn't really set up to allow for an independent run at the White House. Interestingly, the most significant recent successes by third party candidates in the Electoral College were for racists: George

definition forever of what it meant to be a Republican. His definition made me uncomfortable. Trickle-down economics sounded questionable to me, as did Reagan's lurch to the rhetorical right, resulting in someone who sounded far different than the California governor I hadn't perhaps loved but had at least respected.

CB   BO

Last night I had a Twitterdream, yet another sign that my obsession is on the path to redlining. Usually I dream about innocuous things, the kind of things we all dream about, like being naked in public or being chased by some dark figure that turns out to be an amalgamation of your best friend and Sweeney Todd. This time it's more like when I used to dream about work—which would happen a lot. One of the reasons I left Corporatelandia was to reduce those stress levels.

As my wife might say: "How's that workin' for ya?"

In the dream I'm online under my @BeckIsALib persona and it's quite late, perhaps three or four in the morning, a time Sylvia Plath called the blue hour. My home office and bedroom have morphed together so that I'm sitting at my desk before an over-bright monitor while my wife, curled fetally in bed, breathes gently behind me. Both dogs are stretched out on the bed next to her; one of them twitches in her sleep, claiming more and more of the bed's real estate as she does.

Twitter is open and active on my monitor and my timeline speeds along almost faster than I can read. It's really annoying, and I'm starting to get that squishy feeling of oncoming nausea that I some-

---

Wallace received 45 electoral votes in 1968 and Strom Thurmond won 39 electoral votes twenty years earlier.

times get when I try to read my email in the car.[67] The few tweets I do manage to bring into focus are filled with capital-letter shouting and oft-repeated exclamation points. All civility—even as pretense— is gone. I'm getting so frustrated that I come perilously close to slamming my fist down on the keyboard just to make it stop, but there's about as much chance of that happening as there is of Rush Limbaugh retracting the "feminazi" epithets he routinely hurls at The National Organization for Women.

I stare numbly at the screen. My hands are folded together in my lap and I don't even attempt to tweet. What would be the point? I can't imagine ever typing fast enough before what I write becomes meaningless, passed by as thousands and thousands of other tweets move rapidly on to other topics, other rants, other screeds. My voice would be lost in the crowd. Still, after a few more moments and a few thousand more tweets cycle, I feel compelled to try. I will my fingers to the keyboard and command them to type:

BeckIsALib: Can everyone please slow down? I'm trying to get a word in here!

The letters start to fade and float away from the screen even as I type them, mocking me the way that the Ghostly Trio of Fatso, Fusso, and Lazo used to mock Casper the Friendly Ghost, with a weightlessness that drifts into invisibility.

I scramble for the words and images that might startle everyone at once, something that would make everything stop just long enough for my thoughts to be heard. But all I can think of are clichés: Martin Luther King, Jr. shouting about dreams, Patrick Henry screaming about liberty and death, Rodney King pondering the

---

[67] As a passenger, of course. My wife does most of the driving. She's both a better driver and a worse passenger than I am, so it works out well for both of us.

difficulties of cooperation. Emulating the definition of insanity, I try again:

BeckIsALib: Can everyone please slow down? I'm trying to get a word in here!

As before, I'm loudly ignored.

The Twitterstream becomes audible now, sounding like the bastard child of Brian Eno and Pantera. It isn't pretty and I can't shut it off. I glance back over my shoulder. My wife is still asleep, though given the cacophony I don't know how.

The timeline's speed increases to the point where I can't make out a single word through the blur of pixels rushing vertically and away. Feeling like an extra in a cyberpunk novel, I half-expect to dissipate along with the bits and bytes, but, moved by desperation, I give it one more try:

BeckIsALib: Can't you all see that I'm right? That I have the answers? Please slow down and listen...You're really starting to piss me off...

Still nothing. I turn off the computer and let the blackness and silence overtake the room. I listen to my own heartbeat, consciously move it back down from my throat into my chest, and then take a deep breath. I turn again to look at my wife and dogs, but they're not where they were a moment earlier. Instead my wife is standing and looking quietly out the window. She has a dog sitting silently at each side of her, one to the right and one to the left, guardian-like, also staring straight ahead. At this moment I feel impotent. I wonder what I'm doing here, wonder if I—or anyone—can ever impress civility back into our national dialogue. In a world that absorbs thoughts before they're even completed and where there are a million angry screamers for every Victor Mooney, my hope seems childish.

I turn back to the keyboard where the computer has restarted of its own accord, tweets flashing, sounds blaring. My sense of humor is gone; I'm invested.

One more deep breath prefaces my fingers again hitting the keys:

BeckIsALib: We have a responsibility to ourselves, our children, our country, and our world. Our responsibility is to engage reasonably, to think logically, to understand that we all want the same thing, a place where happiness is possible, opportunity is real, and our loved ones are safe. We allow ourselves to be emotionally manipulated by those who don't care about what we care about and who can't be bothered to treat us with respect. We should all be insulted; we should demand more; we should respect ourselves and each other more.

I hit the "Tweet" button. I know I've sent many more than 140 characters, but I am naively hopeful that someone will find it, someone will read it.

WEEK SEVEN:
I BLAME ARISTOTLE

Something's not right.

It's the middle of spring and yet the cameras catch revelers cavorting in Times Square. Cheering crowds line the streets of Boston, Los Angeles, and Omaha. It's the same on every channel: noise, excitement, celebration.

Bold-fonted headlines explain: sometime late last evening (after much of the east coast had tucked itself into bed) a tight team of U.S. Navy Seals tracked down and killed Osama Bin Laden. Each television crawl repeats the same story: at a not terribly well-hidden villa in Pakistan, a bullet to the head culminated a razor-sharp mission, ending Bin Laden's life.

Nearly ten years have passed since the 9/11 attacks, and for just one moment we all stand before our televisions and watch in surprise and pleasure. Many of us were never sure this day would come. Many of us, too, were likely surprised at just how good it felt. For one brief moment American dialogue was absent a right and left, an us and them. There was just the news: the stunning, unbelievable, thought-it-would-never-happen news. I had awoken to a true moment of shock and awe, a moment of closure for the entire country.

Keith Urbahn, chief of staff for former Secretary of Defense Donald Rumsfeld, originally broke the rumor on—where else?—Twitter:

KeithUrbahn: So I'm told by a reputable person they have killed Osama Bin Laden. Hot damn.

Less than an hour later this came from the White House:

Whitehouse: President Obama: "I can report to the American people and to the world, that the U.S. has conducted an operation that killed Osama bin Laden."

The silent togetherness lasted all too briefly. In the Twitterverse only a thin line separates the news from the noise, and the spin started revolving even before the story hit its character limit. Talking heads were scurrying about in preparation for a long spin cycle, lining up pundits, experts, respectful responses, and non-respectful responses to the responses. By the time I sat scanning my timeline, an endless stream flowed, ready and waiting to be read. Many were dignified and respectful, like this one, again from Keith Urbahn:

KeithUrbahn: Appreciate all the RT's and props, but this moment belongs to Pres. Obama and the thousands who dedicated careers and lives to this fight.

Other political figures found grace more difficult. Former Vice President Dick Cheney (a man who enjoyed five military deferments) offered congratulations to the soldiers but stopped short of offering any credit to the White House. A pro-Obama tweeter immediately launched a missile Cheney's way:

NeedCoffee: Good to hear five-deferment Cheney salute our troops but make no mention of the President who ordered the strike.

While the left spent most of its collective Twitterbreath on self-congratulation (along with the occasional "we-got-him-and-you-didn't" schoolyard taunt), the right wasted no time going on offense, the first shots targeting President Obama.[68] For one particular listing tweeter, nothing at all had changed:

ProIsraelite: Just watched Obama's bin Laden address. Could he possibly have said "I," "me," or "at my direction" more times?

Reading the Obama potshots grew dull rather quickly. Not so with those of the doubters, who lined up like covered wagons heading out on the Conspiracy Trail.

Conspiracy theories have a long and often strange history, and emerge from our need to create patterns and meaning from our experiences, often resulting in emotional and irrational beliefs. Many take it way too far. These are people who spend their days wondering if the twenty-three different sections of Obama's Kenyan birth certificate are really just digitally encoded clues that were at one time embedded in the floor of the Library of Congress as part of an Illuminati plot to create a New World Order, such Order originally designed by a cabal jointly headed by the Rothschilds, Sean Penn, George Soros, the managing editor of *The New York Times*, and the ghost of Woodrow Wilson.

---

[68] In arguably the most ironic typo I've ever seen, the crawl on Fox News read "Reports: Obama bin Laden dead." I'm sure it was a mistake; nobody could be that brazen.

Our country has a long and not-so-proud tradition of such folly, an ever-growing subgenre of American mythology that has found its megaphone on Twitter.

> Lovesthesouth: "Bin Laden shot in the head" - US official. Great. Show me the hole.

@Lovethesouth wants to see the body with the bullet hole and the responsible Navy Seal standing over the corpse. He's terribly suspicious that the body was buried at sea and won't accept the reason—insuring that we leave no burial site, no shrine that might become a tool for propaganda. But that means no body and that @Lovethesouth can't abide. He wants the corpse, and not neatly, and he wants to have eighteen separate experts validate the DNA and the dental records and the video footage and the still photos in order to make sure none of it's been doctored, disguised, or manipulated. Even then all of that evidence won't be enough for him.

I expect tweets like @Lovethesouth's to grow more frequent, but for now, with the story just getting started, the crazies and the cranks remain the minority, ceding the landscape to those who are elated, proud, thankful, and sometimes even funny:

> PoughkeepsieDan: They should have captured Bin Laden alive and made him continually go through airport security for the rest of his life....

I wish I had written that. It's really quite clever.

Several people offered intelligent, thoughtful tweets. One even dared to question whether we weren't pretending that with Osama's death things would really be any different:

Gallsworthy: The conditions which spawned bin Laden remain:
Western support for Israel, imperialist occupation, and propping up
of Muslim dictators.

From this tweet I can't tell whether @Gallsworthy is on the right
or the left, but one thing is clear: he has not fallen into the trap of
thinking the problem has gone away. Whether or not one agrees with
him, it's clear that @Gallsworthy understands the symbolic importance of bin Laden's downfall, but also that one man's death does not
an enemy defeat. Rarely do we see that kind of systemic thinking in
our highly polarized dialogues. It takes too much work. We're a
country that needs a bad guy, a simple, easy-to-describe tough in a
black hat that we can all point to and then yell "Get him!" at the top
of our lungs. We're good and they're bad. In our country there is no
room for gray despite the fact that *everything* is gray.

I blame Aristotle.

Aristotle, one of the big three of ancient Greek philosophy (along
with Plato and Socrates), thought and taught about nearly every
branch of the physical and metaphysical sciences, from biology to
ethics, from logic to politics. Alexander the Great studied under him.
For more than two millennia Aristotle's ideas have colored the
scientific lenses through which we view the world. A brilliant man,
no doubt, was our Aristotle. He knew everything, saw everything,
conceived of everything. I imagine he wasn't much fun at parties.

"So, Ari, is it? What do you do for a living?"

"I ponder and pontificate on the great questions: the meaning of
life, the size of our universe and our place in it, the structure of our
bodies and our world. I study everything, from the smallest iota of
matter to the vast and great stars that circle our planet."

"Uh huh. Wow. Gee. How 'bout them Yankees?"

The problem for those of us now swimming a couple of thousand
years downstream is that when someone brilliant makes a mistake it

often takes a long time to change anyone's mind about it. Who are we to doubt someone of such stature? In the physical sciences, for example, we now know that Aristotle's theories of medicine and biology managed to kill people well into the fourteenth century and beyond. He also had a completely geocentric view of the universe and tried to use pure reason to invalidate any observations that disagreed with his preconceived notions.

Philosophies about the physical world, however harsh and long-term their implications, are sooner or later correctable through careful and thoughtful science. Not so with metaphysical philosophies. Those, when passed down from generation to generation, century to century, eventually become part of the cultural DNA. That's what happened to us with Aristotle's metaphysical worldview, a worldview based on duality, the concept of this and that, black and white, yes and no. Dualistic thinking now permeates the Western world, infected along the way by our penchant for sound bites, quick answers, and knee-jerk reactions.

Aristotelian dualism comes from our classic confusion over mind and body. We've simply never been able to get our head around how the two are different, or if they're different at all. Given that dualistic thinking emerged from one of the biggest of the big metaphysical questions,[69] it's not surprising that it managed to double-helix itself into our culture and, in particular, the logical pedestal before which we now lower our heads.

In Aristotle's view of logic, things *are* or *are not*. He scaffolded his thinking with syllogisms, the simplest of which are sets of un-arguable, factual premises that are then used to deduce appropriate conclusions, as in the following example:

---

[69] Just behind "Why are we here?" but well ahead of "Why did they let Seth Rogen play the Green Hornet?"

A—All men are mammals.

B—Jacob is a man.

Therefore, C—Jacob is a mammal.

Such a construct is nice, clean, and straightforward, and you can easily extend the syllogism quite simply:

A—All men are human beings.

B—All human beings are mammals.

C—Jacob is a man.

Therefore, D—Jacob is a mammal.

The problem with Aristotelian logic, however, is that it is limited by two very important yet oft-ignored subtleties. The first is the implied binary nature of the syllogisms; that is, something is or is not. The "something" is never both. It is "either/or," not "both/and." This "either/or" construction is buried so deep in our collective psyche that it is pretty much the only way we know how to think and, in an annoyingly recursive irony, we can't even question the way we think because we can't really conceive a "both/and" to our "either/or" way of thinking.[70]

It's not that way everywhere. There are other ways to think. In many Eastern cultures "both/and" thinking is quite common. Thinking processes in Japan, for example, focus on creating harmony between and among objects rather than automatically separating and categorizing them, tendencies that inhabit the Western mind.

The second oft-forgotten principle is that premises must be facts. In the two examples given above the setups were truths: Men are mammalian; men are human beings. This axiom—that premises be

---

[70] Jeremy Bentham, the English philosopher and reformer, once famously said, "There are two types of people in the world. Those who divide the world into two types and those who do not."

facts—is what makes Aristotle's system of logic work. The problem creeps in when we decide (as with that eleventh-grade history report) that our beliefs are the facts. Even within the limitations of "either/or" thinking, Aristotle's constructs can still work if we would just stick with the facts, yet we often seem unwilling to bother with them, particularly when it comes to politics. I guess it's just too much effort to look things up and perhaps get a second, confirming source. Using beliefs is just so much faster.

Beliefs, though, gum up the works. When you combine our "either/or" DNA with the "belief/fact" confusion that arises from our emotional responses to political issues, what you get are absurdities like this one:

A—All Democrats are libtards.
B—James Carville is a Democrat.
Therefore, C—James Carville is a libtard.

Set aside for a moment how you feel about James Carville and his potential for libtardiness and look only at the construct; the problem should be obvious. Premise "A" is not a fact in the Aristotelian sense. The statement "All Democrats are libtards" is a belief. The statement is not of the same class as, say "the sun rises in the east." No matter how much you might believe in the existence of libtards as somewhat scaly, left-leaning neo-Marxists with bad hair and Ivy League degrees, you still just believe.[71] You can even believe that it's a fact, but that doesn't make it a fact; it's still just a belief. Reduce such thinking to 140 characters and you end up with idiocy like this:

---

[71] For the record, James Carville went to Louisiana State. George W. Bush went to Yale and Harvard. Ann Coulter went to Cornell. You may recognize the names of those last three schools. If you've ever seen pictures of them, you probably noticed the ivy.

MNRepVoter: If federal spending creates jobs, we should have
38% more jobs now than we did in 2006.

While all of @MNRepVoter's points may be true, there's only
one possible fact buried in all that belief and it's hidden like a
randomly drawn frying pan in a *Highlights* hidden picture. It's the
assertion that federal spending ballooned thirty-eight percentage
points since 2006.[72] Beyond that her tweet fails Aristotely, reduced to
her beliefs: that federal spending doesn't create jobs (presented
sarcastically), and that, therefore, we must have wasted all that
money. How do you discuss the legitimacy of such an argument (in
140-character snippets, no less) when the gut so clearly beats the
brain?

Beliefs are very powerful; they move mountains (literally as with
the Transcontinental Railroad), they build bridges (metaphorically, as
with many non-denominational churches), and they impact elections
(maliciously, as with John Kerry and the Swift Boat debacle).
Regardless of that power, beliefs are not facts. Unfortunately, too
many people treat them as if they are. Combine "belief/fact"
conflation with "either/or" thinking and you get stone-headed
stubbornness, sometimes tinged with a bit of crazy. And it comes at
you from anywhere and everywhere, most particularly when someone
wants to sell you something.

In the early days of the Iraq War, President Bush famously said,
"Either you are with us, or you are with the terrorists." Most people
interpreted that statement as meaning, "If you don't support our
policies and our reasons, then you support the terrorists." Those
policies and reasons included an almost metaphysical belief in what

---

[72] Turns out even that "fact" is wrong. Here's what the official government reports
show: the 2006 budget landed at $3.028 trillion while the 2011 budget came in at
$3.834 trillion, for an increase of $806 billion, or 26.6 percent. I was really, really
hoping someone would have their data straight before shooting off another 140-
character falsehood. It might have partially offset the fact that the logic sucks.

were clearly not facts: Iraq's weapons of mass destruction, a connection between Saddam Hussein and 9/11, the need for secret prisons and rendition, and the "understanding" that waterboarding wasn't really torture, but that even if it was, it was okay because it helped us get the guys in the black hats before they got us.

I remember at the time thinking that Bush's statement sounded foolish; clearly I could believe many things other than those two options. I could (and did) believe that invading a sovereign nation was fundamentally wrong, particularly given the absence of a precipitating event. I could (and did) believe that supporting the troops didn't mean supporting the war. And I could (and did) believe that we knee-jerkingly overreacted. Bush's jingoistic Zen koan (soon found echoing on every news and pseudo-news show) meant that no one had to think too deeply; they just had to choose up sides, the adult equivalent of one schoolyard kid yelling at another, "You're stupid," and then waiting for the unending sequence of am-nots and are-toos until, finally, the bell rings to end recess and everyone grudgingly step-marches back into their respective classrooms.

My view doesn't fit well with our Aristotelian DNA. My view acknowledges a middle ground, a way of looking through rather than at. As a country, we're not very good at such thinking. It's not that I prefer the middle ground—sometimes one side or another is right, after all—but I definitely prefer the thoughtful ground.

ભ ૭

I'm now "somebody" on Twitter. In terms of influence and activity, I am nearing the top 15 percent of all tweeters worldwide. Klout now classifies me as a "Specialist," a clear upgrade from my previous status as a mere "Explorer." I have approximately 300 followers and my tweets are regularly retweeted. Klout claims that I influence the thinking of 116 other people. I don't know how Klout reaches that belief or, if true, exactly how such influence might manifest. I just know that it sounds impressive.

Despite this growing influence, I seem stuck in a Twitterpool, a small eddying circle of people and ideas that keeps me pretty well sucked in. I've tried to break out of it with a few off-topic tweets about the Boston Bruins and my fondness for offbeat literature, but I'm not having much luck. I've done well in widening the pool, but it's still the same pool, just a bit broader and deeper. Yesterday, however, I stumbled upon the "jackass" technique.

I saw a tweet that I didn't understand, a reply to someone where the text of the tweet was simply, "I don't really appreciate that." Nosiness and temptation, the *sine qua non* for all Twitter users, sat phrased before me and, since I've never been one to pass up such an opportunity, I decided to follow Twitter's siren call. I expanded the conversation in HootSuite and saw that there were some eight or ten back-and-forths, the tweets largely filled with snark and name-calling. And then it hit me: the conversation's participants were mentioning each other with every exchange. Since mentions are a key Kloutian currency, these people were inadvertently using their shared nastiness to acquire small but real influence bumps. Perhaps if I could carefully pick and choose where to tweet some artful bits of nastiness I, too, could benefit from this statistical loophole.

The technique bubbled with promise and, since there's no shortage of nastiness in the Twitterverse, I figured that my bantam-weight additions wouldn't change the gravitational field one iota. I might piss off one or two people, but that I could deal with. I did not want to insult people's core beliefs, however; that could lead to a backlash of de-following. While my follower count grew daily, it still needed a carefully tended petri dish in which to grow; too much nastiness could quickly lead to ostracism and all cultivations would quickly atrophy, leaving me tweepless and without any influence at all. That would not be good.

I decided to launch a new series of harmless yet provocative tweets: Stupid Regulations. The premise was simple; I'll hunt for regulations that seem like a waste of time and money and then tweet about them in the hope that I might twang a nerve-ending somewhere. A bit of back and forth between tweeps will give me the influence boost I'm looking for, and then I'll move on before anybody gets too peeved about whatever it is we're arguing about. I'll add a new tag while I'm at it—#StupidReg—and see if that helps me get the attention I'm looking for.

I started with a tweet about the signs that every hotel puts up, the ones that hang on the inside of each room door, the ones that no one ever reads. It's true that the signs have directions to the nearest fire exit (in case, in the event of a hotel fire, you choose to read the plastic laminated tiny print on the door as opposed to, say, simply running out into the hallway and looking for the giant, vibrantly red EXIT sign or, even more simply, just looking for smoke and flames and sprinting in the opposite direction), but the signs also have an eye test's worth of contractual language pertaining to your stay, sometimes mated to a list of maximum allowable room rates that are always about eight times what you're actually paying. These notices are a waste of regulatory time and energy; I can only imagine the Monty Python skit in which someone decided they were a good idea.

I key-scribbled my thoughts, making sure to phrase my tweet as a question in order to encourage responses, and then hit the "Tweet" button next to the character counter above my timeline...

BeckIsALib: #Stupidreg: Why do we still need the card on every hotel room door that states the "maximum allowable room rates?"

...and was rewarded with needle-dropping silence. I felt like a talentless heckler at a comedy club who can't even manage to draw attention to himself.[73]

Ever indefatigable, I quickly followed with #StupidReg number two, which addressed regulations for restaurant employee hand-washing. My argument here was simple: since food-borne illness will likely deter an establishment's clientele, why do we need regulation? Self-interest, free-market forces, and a little common sense should take care of the issue.

> BeckIsALib: #StupidReg: Do we really need to regulate handwashing behavior for restaurant employees? Won't the owners WANT to stay open?

The reaction, from one @GillyBlack, was much stronger than I expected. Apparently the talentless heckler had woken someone up. Maybe the belligerent tone did it.

> GillyBlack @BeckIsALib Yeah, leave the damn restaurant owners alone. I want to get hepatitis! Also, quit worrying if your surgeon wears gloves!!

Then, even before I responded to his response, @GillyBlack was at me again:

> GillyBlack @BeckIsALib If you are looking for an issue with legs, restaurant handwashing ain't it!! #StupidRegsthatSaveLives

---

[73] Side note: I actually *was* a talentless heckler at a comedy club once, way back in the mid-seventies. Fueled by liquor, I was enjoying the mad antics of a hilarious up-and-comer named Robin Williams. He ate me for lunch.

Cleary the guy's a bit irritated; he's even added his own hash tag, a variation on my #StupidReg. I don't much care. Every mention boosts my influence and my newfound "jackass mode" appears to be working: Gilly and I are engaged. Not willing to let go of a good thing, I keep tweeting:

BeckIsALib: @GillyBlack My point was that it's just so obvious! And unenforceable!

GillyBlack: @BeckIsALib No it is not. To most employees that are told "it is the law," that carries weight over "do it because the boss said so."

I happen to disagree with Gilly, but it doesn't really matter. Count the mentions: four quick ones in about five minutes or so; that's what I call Twitterfficiency. Plus, I actually enjoyed our brief chat; his avoidance of character-saving contractions I find quite endearing, along with his way of doubly exclamating a key point.

Notice, too, that there's nary a single sign of real logic in the entire exchange. It's all just belief.

ଔ ଚ

The bastardization of logic—particularly in the service of jackass-dom—is an inherent part of our national dialogue and has been for some time.

I first noticed the trend on a nondescript afternoon nearly twenty years ago while driving along Route 46 in Parsippany, New Jersey. Having just left work for the day, I grumbled to myself about the traffic and listened with half an ear to Rush Limbaugh, as elitist a conservative as one could ever imagine.[74]

Though pompous, Limbaugh is also at times amusing (and even informative). I've always had a bit of a love/hate relationship with his show; he possesses a laudable willingness to talk about things that others don't talk about and is amazingly articulate, but at the same time he manages to patronize his callers—even the ones who agree with him. Back in the early nineties he even seemed reasonable at times while still somehow managing to emit the strident hyperbole of the far right. At his best, he is cogent and thoughtful; at his worst, he embodies every GOP caricature rolled into one: the overweight, cigar-smoking rich man in an expensive suit that spends his time bitching and moaning about the lower classes, bringing to mind nothing so much as the guy in the middle of the Monopoly® board.

That particular drive home down that particular crowded highway listening to that particular radio program has stuck with me all these years. Why? The reason is simple: it's the day I realized that Rush Limbaugh thought I was incredibly stupid and, therefore, easily manipulated.

Rush was blow-hardily pontificating on the evils of sex, the crashing morals of (then) today's generation, and the risk of AIDS. His argument centered on the arguably false security provided by condoms with respect to preventing the disease. Rush explained that condoms were 90 percent effective, and went on to liken having sex with a condom to flying in an airplane. He then rhetorically asked whether any of us would fly in an airplane if we knew it had a 10

---

[74] Limbaugh claims to have his "talent on loan from God." The statement strikes me as odd since I usually think of God as a Being of infinite gifts, not loans. Limbaugh makes God sound too much like the neighbor who wants to borrow my hedge trimmer. However, if Limbaugh is right and God did loan him talent, then he should have asked for a bigger loan.

percent failure rate. If not, he went on, why would we ever trust our lives to a condom? It's the same thing, he said.

Well, no. It's not.

I don't recall exactly what happened next in the real world—it was about twenty years ago, after all—but in the world of metaphor steam poured out of my ears, my jaw dropped to my knees, and the words "Blammo!" and "Kapow!" floated three-dimensionally just above the steering wheel. There were just so many flaws in his logic that I couldn't believe that *he* could believe what he was saying.

The crater-sized gaps in his argument took no time to find. First, the basic facts seemed a bit fuzzy; I didn't have the information at my fingertips, but for some reason I thought the failure rate of condoms was much lower than 10 percent, perhaps more like 2 percent.[75] Even if I accept his 1-in-10 statistic, the analogy still crumbles. Let's start from the end of the argument: one's willingness (or unwillingness) to fly on an airplane if 10 percent of them insist on listening to gravity's call. Well, it doesn't take a genius to see that the fatality rate of such an event would be pretty near 100 percent. But that's not the case with the front end of the analogy. If, as Rush (and the Catholic Church, by the way) claim, 10 percent of condom-centric sex ends in condom failure,[76] it certainly doesn't mean a 100 percent fatality rate for those so affected. In order for that to be true it would mean that 100 percent of sex events had at least one partner with HIV, that 100 percent of HIV-related sex events resulted in HIV-transmission, and that 100 percent of HIV transmissions resulted in death. Even if I

---

[75] Turns out that the failure rate is roughly between 0.5 percent and 2.3 percent but, in fairness to Rush, that's a perfect use failure rate. Given that some people tend to be a bit sloppy about it (i.e., use the damn things imperfectly), Rush's 10 percent estimate probably isn't that far off.

[76] Actually, I doubt they would actually *end* in condom failure. More likely condom failure would happen somewhere in the middle and the participants would keep on going. I know I would.

ignore this last point and allow that HIV will eventually lead to full-blown AIDS and then to death (generally believed true at the time), the logic still doesn't work.

In the early nineties an estimated 0.3 percent of the adolescent and adult U.S. population suffered from HIV[77] and the rate of transmission in unprotected (or failed-condom) sex was, at most, 10 percent. Rush's math was all wrong because his facts were all wrong (or simply absent from his argument completely, likely because they were inconvenient truths). The real math says that a 10 percent condom failure rate (which I'll accept) multiplied by a 0.3 percent chance that my partner has HIV (and, yes, I know that I've smoothed out the demographic differences here for simplicity's sake, but it's not a big difference), multiplied by the maximum 10 percent chance that any unprotected exposure results in transmission means that I don't have a 1-in-10 chance of dying, I have a 3-in-10,000 chance of probably dying from AIDS at some time in the future. That's 0.0003 percent, or roughly equivalent to the likelihood that I'll die of accidental drowning.

I'll acknowledge that it's still more dangerous than flying in an airplane (1-in-20,000 chance of dying), but if you give the average young male odds of 3-in-10,000 in exchange for a brief tumescent explosion, my guess is that he's taking his chances. As a persuasive argument, Rush, you've got nothing to work with here.

More importantly, how could Limbaugh possibly think I was that dumb? I learned how to think this way in the fifth grade back when Mrs. Levy was handing out purple dittos printed with word problems that asked me stupid questions about the speed of trains relative to

---

[77] As reported in a July 1996 article in *JAMA*, the *Journal of the American Medical Association*. Of course the citation is only valid if you believe that science has any credibility at all, as opposed to, say, believing that facts result from the steroidal injection of public opinion into the body politic.

fleet-footed gazelles.[78] If I could figure it out, then certainly Rush Limbaugh, given all that talent on loan from God, could figure it out as well. He just didn't want to. It didn't serve his purpose. On top of that, he apparently assumed that his listeners were either so blindly loyal or so exceedingly stupid[79] that they wouldn't know or care about his obvious manipulations.

Was that really all he was about, all he is about? Is that really all anyone with a political agenda is about? Is everyone out there—right or left—trying to snow me with idiocy and temporary talent?

CR BO

What does it mean when your own behavior makes you queasy?

Just a couple of weeks ago I considered myself a model of civility. Except for those few SHOUTING episodes and the occasional sardonic belch, I generally think of myself as a calmer voice than most. It's hard, after all, not to mix your tone with those around you, especially if you want to be heard. Humor gets retweets; brashness gets attention. I've simply fit in well. But then I realized that buried within the whole "jackass technique" there lies a troll, one that cares not for either the angel or the devil sitting on my shoulders. He simply swats them away and marches west to east then east to west like some medieval homunculus keeping watch for any possible sign of sanity.

Victor Mooney sets the standard and it's one I haven't lived up to.

---

[78] The questions didn't seem quite so stupid at the time, probably because we were all having a blast sniffing the purple ink on the dittos; the active chemical was spirit ether.

[79] For those of you ready to accept this conclusion, it's not true. Based on analysis of visitors to Rush's website and research from Pew, more than half of his audience arrives college educated. He does have a demographic problem, though; his audience skews heavily to elderly white males, as does Beck's.

ReaganStyle: I want a President who will bring the troops home. Do we really need to be fighting six undeclared & unconstitutional wars?

ReaganStyle: Undeclared wars, torture, secret arrests, crumbling liberties, income taxes, central banking...Are we a Republic?

ReaganStyle: You can be spiritual without being religious.

Victor, as I've mentioned, disagrees with me on quite a few things, and he's as inclined as anyone else to present beliefs as facts. But look again at the tweets above. There's nary a snark among them: no calls for impeachment, no hidden desire to burn heretics: just respectful opinion. Victor engages with thousands of others while only rarely raising his virtual voice. He never looks for a skirmish. If he happens to step into one, he stays calm, often using humor to diffuse the mood. He's like a musician with 10,000 hours of practice; he models appropriate Twitterquette as second nature.

I, on the other hand, definitely need more practice:

BeckIsALib: It's bizarre that when a leftist actor talks politics we want them to shut up but people swallow swill from Chuck Norris.

BeckIsALib: I wonder how many backyard barbecues will include "Kool-Aid" today? Seems like people are drinkin' a lot of it lately...

And, in perhaps the worst display of all, a tweet in response to an ardent pro-life supporter who made the erroneous claim that nearly one-quarter of all abortions lead to complications (including miscarriages) in subsequent pregnancies:

BeckIsALib: @TooManyDie: Your numbers are wildly wrong, but thanks for playing.

That's just not like me. Most of my friends would probably say that while I love to win an argument and am never above a bit of sarcasm, I am, at heart, a nice person. You couldn't tell it from what I've been tweeting lately. There's no wit, no sign of intention. Just snark.

In his short book *Snark: It's Mean, It's Personal, and It's Ruining Our Conversation*, David Denby calls snark "a strain of nasty, knowing abuse spreading like pinkeye through the national conversation." Apparently I've begun making my contributions.

WEEK EIGHT:
ELECTILE DYSFUNCTION

Yesterday Newt Gingrich announced his intention to announce his intention to run for president. Gail Collins, in a
New York Times article, said of this, "I don't think I've been
this excited since last week when a guy came to read our gas meter."

The presidential election cycle in this country lasts a bit over two
years, ridiculous for a temp job that lasts only four. It means that a
large chunk of us spend half our lives getting all worked up over who
gets to sit in the round room and play with the fancy buttons. It's
not this way everywhere; many other countries manage to select their
leaders in just a few months. Only in America do we parade our
presidential candidates before a series of infinitely projected fun-
house mirrors long enough to ensure that everyone has the opportunity to create their own skewed images.

Ironically, the president doesn't even affect most of us all that
much. Apart from the power to nominate Supreme Court justices,
the position owns the bully pulpit but not much more. The president
only suggests laws and proposes budgets, relying on the legislative
branch to spend or save or tax or allocate. He doesn't hand down
precedent-setting judgments or do more than offer predictable
opinions on constitutionality: that's the judiciary's job. It's true that

the president often signs broad executive orders[80], but it's also true that the next president can undo it all with the equally florid strokes of an autopen. So what's the big deal? It all comes back to figure-heads, finger-pointing, and our need to either laud or blame.

The president is the only elected official whose constituency is all of us, not some demographic segment. He's the guy we put in the saddle, then we sit back and watch as half of the country puts a white hat on his head while the other half imagines him in black. It's nice and it's neat, and it allows us to avoid having the hard debates about how our country works—or doesn't.

In our country election-watching (and the associated polling, posturing, and punditry) is probably second only to baseball as a national pastime.[81] A quick search in the Twitterverse for "2012 election" brings up a sampling from thousands and thousands of recent tweets—and keep in mind that we're still eight months from the earliest primary.

MichaelCottonwood: So excited for the 2012 election, campaign, debates, etc. :)

Sometimeblogger: "Mike Huckabee 2012 Run Looking More Likely," Key supporter says.

Georgiarepry: Newt Gingrich In Georgia—"2012 Presidential Election Most Important Since Before Civil War."

---

[80] Recent presidents have issued, on average, about two or three executive orders a month. In the first three years of his presidency, Obama's average is almost exactly the same as Bush's before him; both are lower than Clinton's.

[81] Except in Texas, where it's way, way behind high school football, and Vermont, where it understandably lags behind public nudity.

Newt's pre-entrance into the race certainly raises the noise level in my particular corner of the Twitterverse, and most of the cacophony skews decidedly anti-Newt. Joan Didion, a brilliant essayist with an acerbic wit, once said of him, "absent an idea that can be sold at Disney World, he has tended to lose interest" and has suggested that he thinks "in outline form, with topic points capitalized."[82] But Gingrich was a force in the party and, given that history, the lack of support must surely disappoint him. Having never been a fan myself, the negative responses actually give me a little hope for the GOP. Intellectual blather is still blather, Newt.

I have Newt to thank, though, for establishing my credentials as a Twitterwit. Gingrich has always seemed rather gnomish to me: he has that Pillsbury face, an overly soft frame and a googly-eyed grin. I decided to call him "Gnewt the Gnome" and I started tweeting it that way. Don't know why. It just seemed funny to me.

I first used the nickname in a friendly back-and-forth that started with @JoanofHart introducing me to a new hash tag: #NewtSlogans. @JoanofHart is pretty far to the left. She's also clever, respectful, and always fun to chat with. She's no Newt fan, as a pair of early #NewtSlogans showed, both centered on Newt's somewhat checkered history with women:

JoanofHart: #NewtSlogans "Adultery – it's for adults."

JoanofHart: #NewtSlogans "Lovin' my country all night long."

Since I love to play, I came back with this one:

---

[82] Both quotes from Ms. Didion's marvelous essay, "Newt Gingrich, Superstar," written in 1995 but all the more resonant today.

BeckIsALib: @JoanofHart: Like your new hash tag.
#NewtSlogans "PowerPoint your way to the Presidency."

She complimented me and then I responded with:

BeckIsALib: @JoanofHart: Thanks. Gnewt the Gnome is not my
favorite candidate, as you can tell. I think I'd stay home rather than
vote for him.

Apparently the "Gnewt" label caught her fancy because the retweets and mentions quickly spiked faster than anything I'd yet tweeted. There's ego gratification in reading something like this:

Oregonlady9: @BeckIsALib: Thanks, my friend. I agree with all
those other folks-- #Gnewt is frikkin' brilliant!

I particularly liked the reference to "all those other folks." So thanks, Gnewt.

Newt Gingrich is only one name on a long list that I've dubbed the Loser's Lineup, a train of names consisting of those who would haplessly attempt the unseating of a sitting president.

Incumbents rarely lose and when they do it's usually for one of three reasons. The first is what I call the "Who Principle." The Who Principle says that when a sitting VP gets the top spot, the public will often decide that they've met the new boss and he's the same as the old boss. That's what happened to George Bush *père* after eight years of Reagan started to feel like twelve years of Reagan.

The second reason I call the "Riegels Phenomenon." Roy "Wrong Way" Riegels, a football player for the University of California, once picked up a fumble and ran sixty-five yards in the wrong direction, scoring for the opposition Georgia Tech Yellow Jackets in the 1929 Rose Bowl. The Riegels Phenomenon occurs when fate presents an incoming president with an important opportunity and we all watch gape-mouthed as he totally screws it up. Carter is my favorite example. Under Ford things were weakening, with inflation and unemployment both at uncomfortable levels. Ford's fumbling gave Carter the opportunity for an important and impactful presidency, but Carter scooped up the ball and ran the wrong way. Jimmy may have been a brilliant man (by all accounts he was), but as a leader he left a lot to be desired.

The third reason doesn't need a special name; it's the economy, stupid. It's a simple truism that people usually vote their wallets and when things are going well, people tend to embrace their own inertia. When times are harder, we're more likely to vote for a change.

Some believe that Obama may be vulnerable because of today's economic woes;[83] the poll numbers currently show him on the bubble. Still, the GOP hasn't found the kind of dynamic, articulate leader that might make Obama's unseating a reality. There's no Reagan, who wiped out Carter in 1980 and wasn't called "The Great Communicator" for nothing. There isn't even a John McCain-style war hero with folksy charm. One guy I tweet with pretty regularly, @Memphisishome, put it this way:

> Memphisishome: My guess is that Obama is virtually unbeatable in 2012 and the GOP knows it. That is why they are all backing off from taking Obama on.

The Loser's Lineup is long and it's boring, filled with retreads, has-beens, wanna-bes, and can-never-bes, with only the occasional interesting face. Unfortunately, those faces are only interesting in the

---

[83] Not to mention the many who would argue that he's fallen victim to the Riegel's Phenomenon as well, arguably exacerbating an already weakening situation. Only history will have that vote, though. Well...come to think of it...we'll get to vote before history does....

way that Goldwater, Dole, and even Thomas Dewey were interesting: as potential landslide victims awaiting the crush of the electorate.

Only a couple of well-known names appear even minimally viable (though it is still early). Mitt Romney (who made a solid run for the nomination in 2008 but came up short in his attempt to catch John McCain) leads the pack. The tides remain strong for Romney; the GOP has a long history of giving people their turn as the party nominee, particularly after coming close in a previous campaign. Nixon rose from the dead after losing as a sitting vice president, Reagan got the nod after nearly unseating Ford, McCain followed George W. Bush, and now Romney could very well get his shot.

Mitt's primary problem is that he's the Republican nominee that looks most like a Democrat. As governor of Massachusetts Romney signed a health care mandate; his ideas became a blueprint for Obama's health care initiatives and not many people are prepared to let him forget it. He used to be pro-choice and now he's not. He used to support certain forms of gun control and now he doesn't. Some feel he suffers from a flip-flop problem, but that may be too kind. His more aggressive critics suggest he has a pandering problem. In 1994, for example, Romney favored strong gun control laws and said that he "did not line up with the NRA." In 2006—suspiciously near his decision to run for president—he joined the NRA as a lifetime member.

But Republicans tend to forgive their own; that fact—along with his carefully crafted talking points—gives Romney some cover within his own party. But Democrats have learned from men like Karl Rove how to be cruel; they've seen how a good lie or well-placed rumor has destroyed more than one viable Democratic candidate, and I fully expect that Mitt, as the frontrunner, will bear the brunt of that malice.

Plus, he's a Mormon.

I know what you're thinking, but it's all in your own head. There's no bigotry in that four-word sentence, just fact. And beneath it, more facts: a hefty chunk of the Republican base comes from a very passionate portion of the Christian evangelical right;[84] many practicing evangelical Christians consider Mormonism a cult or sect;[85] there are more registered Democrats than Republicans. Therefore, Republicans can't win if they can't motivate the base to come out to the polls, and a portion of that base may not want to come out and vote for a Mormon.

Tim Pawlenty, the former governor of Minnesota, garners some praise here and there as well, appearing to have both the credibility and the credentials to make a serious run.

NHPundit: Tim Pawlenty is looking and sounding very presidential here at Halligan Tavern. Showing knowledge and command on all issues.

Like Romney, Pawlenty governed as a Republican in a traditionally liberal state. A self-proclaimed social conservative who remains consistently pro-life, tough on crime, and against nearly all federal regulation, Pawlenty may be the most authentic Republican candidate on the landscape today—if you only see the very far right of the landscape. He also looks decent in a suit and tie unlike, say, Ron Paul.

---

[84] According to a blog on Christianity, roughly one in four Americans are self-identified as evangelicals and approximately 75 percent of those people vote Republican.

[85] Pastors4Huckabee.com has a blog entitled "7 Questions Christians Must Ask Before Voting for a Mormon." Question 1: "Is Mormonism a false cult that deceives people and leads many to hell?" Answer: "Yes."

Ron is one of several second-tier candidates in the clown parade, all of them climbing over each other in their quest to be first out of the tiny car. Newt is clearly the head clown (though Donald Trump is determined to give Newt a run for his money); he's followed closely by the always-good-for-a-laugh candidates: Sarah Palin, Mike Huckabee, the aforementioned Ron Paul, and Rick "Please Don't Forget Me" Santorum.

Donald Trump's rise, simultaneously baffling and frightening, centers on one particular strategy—getting the kooks all worked up. To do that he's picked a pre-packaged topic, the "birther" conspireacy, in which a very vocal (and arguably crazy) contingent of the right wing continually promotes the debunked rumor that our president wasn't actually born in the United States but rather someplace else like, say, Kenya, thus making him ineligible for the presidency under Article Two, Section One of the U.S. Constitution:[86]

> No person except a natural born Citizen, or a Citizen of the United States, at the time of the Adoption of this Constitution, shall be eligible to the Office of President; neither shall any Person be eligible to that Office who shall not have attained to the Age of thirty-five Years, and been fourteen Years a Resident within the United States.

The most public of public faces for the birther movement continues to be an ordinary looking madcap named Orly Taitz. For quite some time Orly managed to roll through the talk and (pseudo)news shows whenever one of them had three minutes to fill and needed to find an amusing story that didn't involve dogs knocking over toddlers

---

[86] The right, it should be noted, did not originate the idea; there's a fair bit of evidence that the rumors began within the ranks of Hillary Clinton supporters during the 2008 primary season.

on snow sleds. On-call Orly would grab her enormous file of useless and disproven hypotheses, hightail it over to whichever studio (real or virtual) she needed to, dab a little too much eye shadow on, and dutifully make us laugh until milk flew from our noses.

Set aside for a moment why this particular issue arose with this particular president,[87] and just know that the issue has no foundation. Every claim—and there have been dozens—has been refuted, but that still doesn't stop Donald Trump from putting on his Elmer Fudd hat and heading off to go wabbit hunting. Why Trump chose this particular dead-end trail will forever remain a mystery. But give the man credit: he knows how to dominate the airwaves when he wants to.

After a few weeks of this Trumped-up craziness, President Obama decided to silence the distraction once and for all by releasing the oft-requested proof: his long-form birth certificate. Just to be clear: this is the President of the United States we're talking about here. The man has to be one of the most vetted human beings on the planet, yet still he felt compelled to respond in order to silence a pest who happened to have the power to prolong the news cycle.[88]

And there are people out there in the Twitterverse who seriously want this guy to run, like @RampartsGlare, who not only doesn't believe the evidence in the long-form but also believes that Trump suffers from unfair demonization:

---

[87] Hint: strange name and dark skin. But that's just my opinion.

[88] The birther movement continues despite the release of the long-form birth certificate since it's far easier to attack proof than to admit error. As Jonathan Kay points out in *Among the Truthers: A Journey through America's Growing Conspiracist Underground*, hard-core conspiracists are never convinced; facts are either wrong or invented as part of the conspiracy.

RampartsGlare: Not the whole story, yet again - more erroneous info and hypocrisy to try to demonize Trump. Trump for POTUS 2012!

Maybe I should take back what I said before about having a little hope.

Trump's toe-dipping into the candidacy waters (he hasn't even announced to announce at this point) definitely benefits at least one other candidate: Sarah Palin looks positively rational by comparison.

Sarah Palin, perhaps the most polarizing figure in modern American politics that I've seen in my lifetime, brings out extreme adoration and extreme loathing, both unsurprisingly easy to find in the Twitterverse:

NeedPalinNow: Sarah Palin is the Leader that America needs. She is the cure to the disease that has infected DC.

LovetheShow: Palin says she'll announce 2012 plans by the end of summer. I hope she jumps in. The GOP clown car still has some room.

You can love her or hate her, but it's useless to deny that in only four short years she's changed from a backwater nobody into one of the incredibly rich conservative elite with regular speaking gigs, a couple of books, and a television show. She even managed to turn an innocuous, innocent, crowd-pleasing program—*Dancing With the Stars*—into a political circus when her daughter Bristol (A star? Really?) appeared on the show and gamely stepped her way through the cha-cha-cha, foxtrot, and rumba. I'd have to check with Guinness, but I think it may have been the first time a celebrity-filled game show ended up so totally politicized since Marlon Brando refused to accept the Academy Award for *The Godfather*, sending Sacheen Littlefeather to the podium in his place.

Enough has been written about Palin's rise to fill the Roman catacombs, and I'm not going to rehash that history here, other than to share one brief and wonderful quote from Jerry K. Remmers' blog *The Moderate Voice*, posted on January 15, 2011:

> In 2008 Palin was a subprime loan bought by John McCain to bolster his sagging presidential campaign and she eventually spun that into a toxic asset for the Republican Party.
>
> Viewed as a presidential candidate in 2012, even Republicans in high leadership roles are mumbling she is not the real thing for the Oval Office.

Subprime loan. I love that.

As of January 2011, Palin had the highest Q-factor (a measure of celebrity popularity) in all of American politics. Still, a Quinnipiac College poll taken on May 4, 2011 shows that 58 percent of registered voters "would never vote" for Sarah Palin in a general election.

She's a mama grizzly, sure. But that's not my idea of the free world's leader, and the majority of American voters (plus-or-minus four percent) apparently agree with me.

She also carries around the kind of baggage that would make American Tourister proud. Her unmarried teenage daughter went off and became an unmarried teenage mother. She's been caught reading notes off of her hand. She whiffed at the softest of softball questions when she couldn't name a single newspaper or magazine she had read. Her gun-toting, gun-sighting rhetoric links her (albeit unfairly) to the shooting of Arizona Representative Gabrielle Giffords. All this and more puts her in the Democratic crosshairs.

And then there are all of those wonderful quotes:

'Refudiate,' 'misunderestimate,' 'wee-wee'd up.' English is a living language. Shakespeare liked to coin new words too. Got to celebrate it!

But obviously, we've got to stand with our North Korean allies.

As Putin rears his head and comes into the air space of the United States of America, where– where do they go? It's Alaska. It's just right over the border.

And my absolute favorite:

I want to help clean up the state that is so sorry today of journalism. And I have a communications degree.

In complete contrast to Palin and her never-ending stream of mainstream media "gotcha" moments, Mike Huckabee presents as an articulate, intelligent, somewhat soft-spoken and kindly man. I met Huckabee very briefly at a campaign stop he made during his 2008 run; what I remember most about him is that he was shorter than I expected.

As nice as he seems, Huckabee, a former Southern Baptist minister, is about as right as one can get without serving as pastor of the Westboro Baptist Church. He would outlaw all abortions, period, and has suggested that American has gone "from Barney Fife to Barney Frank." He also (albeit briefly) jumped on the birther train. I give him credit for a social conscience, however: he respects and understands the importance of education, of the spiritual over the material, and of parents as role models. We likely differ on the implementation but I respect his sincerity. He's also quite good with a line; several of his unscripted comments reveal a wickedly acerbic sense of humor. Comparing himself to Bill Clinton, also from the same hometown, Huckabee said, "I'm from Hope, Arkansas. You may have heard of it. All I'm asking is give us one more chance." He also once suggested that people like him were somewhat rare in Arkansas where a Republican "feels about as out of place as Michael Vick at the Westminster dog show." All of that makes Huckabee someone I respect but don't quite like.

Huckabee may not even join the race given that he has a very lucrative gig as a Fox News talking head. We won't have to wait long to find out; tonight he plans to give us a hint during—wait for it—his Fox News talking head show. Many are less than impressed:

Cheerstoall: Guess what I'm gonna be doing tonight? Not giving a rat's ass about whether Huckabee is running in 2012.

Another tweep echoes my own opinion:

FoxTeats: Everybody knows for the love of money Rev. Huckabee is not running in 2012. He is living high off the hog at Fox Propaganda.

The rest of the Loser's Lineup mashes the almost-declared together with the please-declare, the latter being those currently unprepared to take center stage but still cocking one ear toward the recruitment calls. The two most recognizable of these, Chris Christie and Mitch Daniels, currently occupy the governorships of New Jersey and Indiana, respectively. Of the two, Daniels seems more ready to dip a toe in the water, though he's angered the far right by removing the focus from social conservatism and sticking with the economy, stupid. Christie continues to claim that he's not interested, and people are starting to believe him. Still, he's a centrist Republican—at least when compared to most of the other candidates—and might be able to pull some of those historically fickle Reagan Democrats his way.

And finally, sitting up in the cheap seats, are those who have absolutely no qualifications to lead the free world but have nevertheless managed to attract a small circle of ardent appreciators. Herman Cain is the most visible of the lot in my part of the Twitterverse; Twitter campaigning and fundraising rank high on Herman's list of strategic bullet points.

Cain, the former CEO of Godfather's Pizza (and former chair of the Federal Reserve Bank of Kansas City), styles himself the savior of an "American Dream" that is "under attack." He also reminds us that "we must stand by our friends and we must not be fooled by our enemies. We should never be deceived by terrorists. They only have one objective, namely, to kill all of us. We must always remain vigilant in dealing with adversaries." Hard to disagree, but is any of that meaningful? Is anyone thinking, "No, Herman. Sorry. I like being deceived by terrorists. It puts a bit of fun and challenge into the day."

Lately I'm seeing Cain's name in the Twitterverse more than any other candidate's, but despite the noise I'm not sensing any intense emotion one way or the other. It's probably because he continues to make rhetorically vapid statements like this one:

Richsprings: "Real leaders fix stuff, not make stuff worse."
--Herman Cain

Now there's a *bon mot* worth tweeting about.

Someone should inform Herman that politics and business are not the same thing, that CEOs and presidents function very differently. Let's face it: deciding whether the Sunday newspaper insert should have a $1 discount coupon on two cheese pizzas is not quite the same as negotiating currency valuations with the Chinese. The idea of Herman Cain as president is roughly the same as having the Hardy Boys heading up the CIA: fictionally funny at best. Cain at least has a marketing machine that commandeers media time; not so with the bottom of the Loser's Lineup. See if any of these names ring a bell: Gary Johnson, Fred Karger, Vern Wuensche, Tom Miller. They didn't for me; I had to look them up. Gary Johnson is a former governor; given that he has real experience and no name recognition at all he might be the best candidate currently out there. Tom Miller, on the other hand, is a "career flight attendant" who believes that America "is being destroyed from within." He points out that his job has allowed him to visit all fifty states and several other countries, which probably makes him more qualified on foreign and domestic policy issues than Sarah Palin.

❧ ❧

Living in New Hampshire gets me a VIP pass to the carnival whether I want it or not.

I've lived up here just over six years now, and while I'd heard the stories about how crazy the first-in-the-nation primary season can be, description pales next to reality. It's nuts. Every single candidate and almost-candidate lines up to pay us visit after visit after visit. In the early days these treks focus mainly on Manchester, Concord, and Nashua, but as the calendar shifts into midsummer, candidates start popping up in Keene and Peterborough to the west, Portsmouth and Exeter to the east, and Laconia and Berlin to the north. Every cliché shakes off its cobwebs. Hands are pumped and babies suffer kisses. Skiing and hiking become everyone's favorite sports, and a working paper mill suddenly harkens back to the good old hard-scrabble days of yesteryear. All the attention makes us feel pretty important since we know unequivocally that winning a primary in New Hampshire means momentum.

Only not really. Despite our state's inflated sense of self-worth, it turns out that winning the New Hampshire primary doesn't always mean that much. In 2008 Hillary Clinton won on the Democratic side while John McCain won for the Republicans, giving us the same odds of success as someone predicting heads over tails. It's true that John Kerry and Michael Dukakis both won here before heading off to lose for the Democrats, but we also gave the nod to John McCain in the year Bush won the nomination, and to Pat Buchanan the year Bob Dole topped the ticket. Other famous misses include Paul Tsongas and Gary Hart on the Democratic side, and Henry Cabot Lodge (against Goldwater in 1964) on the GOP side. Lodge wasn't even running at the time; we literally scribbled him on to primary victory. With that kind of track record it's not so much pomp-and-circumstance here in New Hampshire, as much as it's just pomp-and-more-pomp. Still, I've heard that the candidate breakfasts at the Red Arrow Diner are fun.

This year marks the beginning of my second New Hampshire primary season. I'm more motivated than usual and have decided to crawl out from behind my @name and see what's happening in the real world. I've just written a twenty dollar check to join my town's Republican Committee, which "exists to promote the policies of the Republican Party, to assist local Republican candidates campaigning for office, to inform the voting public on issues, and to encourage citizens to vote."

Clubs and I have never much gotten along. Introverted to a fault, I just don't seem to fit in well. I'm uncomfortable around new people, hate to shake hands with strangers, and have never developed the conversational skills that make me sound like I sincerely care about what the other person is saying even when I truly do. I'm not proud of it, but there it is and now, on the other side of fifty, I doubt I'll ever change.

Writing the check was the easy part, much easier than getting into my car and actually showing up for my first meeting. Despite my trepidation (and nearly obvious aversion to handshaking), I was warmly welcomed by the current chairman, Jack, a gentle-voiced man wearing khakis, a light jacket, and a broad smile. About fifty chairs were neatly set up in our meeting room, one of three on the lower level of the public library.[89] Tonight only fifteen people showed up, but Jack assured me that the group had a "couple of hundred" dues-paying members and that turnout wasn't usually this light.

The meeting began with the Pledge of Allegiance. Everyone stood, hats or hands over their hearts, and turned slightly to face the American flag standing on the right side of the room. Until that moment I hadn't even noticed it was there. I felt decidedly odd: I hadn't pledged to the flag since grade school, and it felt both awkward and strange. I understand both flag and pledge as important symbols for many people, but I've never internalized either with the kind of devotion that others have. For me it was merely a duty, not much different than standing for *The Star Spangled Banner* at the ballpark. The request to stand and pledge surprised me, and then I felt shame for feeling surprised, and then shame for feeling ashamed.

I originally learned the Pledge of Allegiance around the same time I learned to breathe. In the dawn of the 1960's, when civil rights and Vietnam were still just words to a single mom and two kids living in a series of Los Angeles apartments, no one in my school ever questioned starting each school day with the Pledge. Why would we? We wore uniforms then, too: pale blue shirts and dark sweaters embroidered with the school's patch, and dark pants with shined shoes. During the summer—I went to school year-round through

---

[89] The same library used to pursue my Nobel hunt a few years back. I don't get out much.

the third grade—the dress shirts shifted to red t-shirts with white logos and shorts.

The flag was sacred in our eyes; I knew how to fold it properly before I was six. We learned by practicing on large sheets of brown paper, creating end-over-end triangles and then carefully tucking in the edges to ensure a perfectly symmetrical wedge. A teacher whose name I don't remember but who smelled like Juicy Fruit gum would walk behind us smiling and taking notes. We begged her to entrust us with the flag's daily ascent and descent up and down the school's two-story flagpole and, when finally chosen, we made sure that no edge ever touched the ground, that no smudge ever marked the fabric. Every elementary school day of every elementary school year we stood at attention and pledged to our flag, hands over our hearts, looking just like a *Life* cover photo or a Norman Rockwell painting.

Those memories rose as I stood awkwardly in this room in this basement in this library with fourteen other people, all of them looking like they did this every day, just as I had over forty-five years ago. I remembered what it sounded like back then, the resonance of multiple voices in accidental harmony reciting these words: "I pledge allegiance/to the flag/of the United States of America…" For anyone raised in the middle of the last century, these are powerful sounds.

We sat back down. The moment was over and I scanned the room, wondering how many of these people knew that the words "under God" were not part of the original Pledge, or that the Pledge was written by a socialist, Francis Bellamy, back in 1892.

The meeting proceeded, obeying Robert's Rules. Motions, seconds, and voice votes approved the previous meeting's minutes, the current budget, and the summer's agenda. A few announcements followed, then two visitors, each representing a GOP contender, were given ten minutes each to sell us on their respective candidates. Jessica, a young woman in her early twenties dressed casually and bearing a wide smile, spoke first. She animatedly supported Rick Santorum who, when he was in the Senate, had been entrusted both with the chairmanship of the Senate Republican Conference and with the Candy Desk.[90] His fervent social conservatism bleeds through on virtually every issue; he has come out strongly against homosexuality, immigration reform, and evolution, and he pounds these issues for emotional echoes at every opportunity. Santorum once commented that "if the Supreme Court says that you have the right to consensual [gay] sex within your home, then you have the right to bigamy, you have the right to polygamy, you have the right to incest, you have the right to adultery. You have the right to anything."

Jessica bubbled through her ten minutes, though it was clear from the number of "umms" and "uhhs" that public speaking was still a somewhat new experience for her. She remained cheerful despite the awkwardness, though based on the merely courteous hand-clapping awarded her work, I imagine that Santorum's campaign will fall short here.

Jessica settled back into her seat and Marcus, a young gentleman in business-casual dress, took her place at the podium, hoping to win us over to the cause of Governor Tim Pawlenty.

Marcus distributed handouts covered with "10 Facts About Governor Tim Pawlenty." I learned that he has "extensive experience in international affairs," is a "nationally recognized leader in health care reform," and has "vetoed every tax hike sent to him." The Minnesota Supreme Court "is today a conservative court because of Governor Pawlenty's five judicial appointments." He's generally anti-

---

[90] I kid you not. According to Wikipedia, the Candy Desk "located on the Republican side of the Senate chamber, was first stocked with candy and treats by Senator George Murphy." It has been a Senate fixture since 1968. Wikipedia goes on to say that "the tenant of the candy desk is charged with stocking it with candy from his or her home state, but funding has been an issue." Most of the candy now comes from lobbyists. Santorum favored products from Hershey and Just Born.

union and saves a bit of extra rancor for the teachers. All in all, he's what passes these days for a mainstream Republican.

Marcus received slightly more attention for his guy than Jessica did for hers, possibly because Marcus' talking points flowed more smoothly and he had those visual aids. We here in New Hampshire appreciate a certain casual professionalism and Pawlenty fit the bill, at least so far. Santorum didn't. I felt a bit bad for Jessica.

Next up was our guest speaker, a professor and pollster from the University of New Hampshire. For the next hour our small group enjoyed a well-prepared and entertaining presentation about the makeup of the New Hampshire electorate and what it might mean for this year's crop of GOP candidates. Much of what I heard surprised me. It turns out that New Hampshire Republicans are some of the least conservative Republicans in the nation. In fact, there are whole states where the Democrats are more conservative than the New Hampshire Republicans. I saw several shaking heads at this point, and I wondered if the club's membership reliably reflected the state as a whole or if it were only the more conservative elements that embraced activism. I think I found out at the end of the meeting when Chairman Jack quietly informed me that the University of New Hampshire polls "tended to be a bit liberal."

With his smile broadening once more, Jack quickly changed subjects, letting me know that he was glad I came and reminding me that there would be no meetings in June or July. Instead I could look forward to the big club social in June, a potluck dinner where people were assigned foods to bring based on the first letter of their last names. The event often attracted 150 or so people, he told me. "Bring your wife if you like." Since my last name is early in the alphabet, I assume I'll also be asked to bring an appetizer. I'll have to wait for the email to find out for sure.

As the meeting broke up I drifted toward the door and wondered if I would be back. I knew why I had come—to explore, face to face, some of the ideas I've been exploring virtually—but I hadn't really had that opportunity. The meeting, largely communication rather than conversation, never provided a chance for the discussion of issues or the sharing of opinions. The ninety minutes provided nothing of what I had expected or hoped for.

This was a small yet motivated group of people who really cared about what they were doing, people who had chosen to give time and energy in order to make the world into what they believed would be a better place. Laudable, yes, but did they simply accept the political rhetoric or did they ever talk about it? If only the former, then did I want to be part of it? Could I see myself stepping out of the safe (though often caustic) virtual world of the Twittersphere and actually doing something? I'm beginning to think that maybe I could. Maybe I would. Perhaps if my views challenged the often misnamed "conventional wisdom," then I should be more active, if only to provide a voice, provide balance.

Damn. I'm starting to care.

WEEK NINE:
YOU CAN'T KEEP A DOWN MAN GOOD

America needs its bad guys—the more unambiguously hateful the better—and given a cultural blueprint that predisposes us to think simply, we'll gladly embrace bad-guy rhetoric as long as it's delivered with wit and style. Glenn Beck—for all that I may not like about him—has wit and style in droves. He also knows that when it comes to bad guys, the blacker the hat the better. So thanks (at least in part) to Glenn Beck, Adolph Hitler is enjoying an enormous resurgence.

Hitlerian comparisons have a long history. Back in 2002 Matthew Engel, a writer for the *Guardian*, wrote an essay entitled "Enough with the Hitler Analogies," in which he reminds us that "Saddam Hussein is not Hitler, as hysterical Americans keep claiming," nor is Israel "the mirror image of Nazism." He adds additional comparative absurdities, including George Bush and Tony Blair as modern-day Adolphs. More than a quarter century earlier the Hastings Center (a nonpartisan research institute) convened to discuss the use of Nazi analogies in ethical debate. Ten years after that Hastings was still discussing the habit and issued a report describing how Hitler and

Nazi analogies are often used to secure the moral high ground and thereby stunt any real debate, the rhetorical equivalent of taking Pork Chop Hill before the other guys get there.

Like just about everything else in our Twittercentric universe, mention Hitler and the name echoes like the sound of a water droplet in Mammoth Cave: endlessly. In two months of tweeting I'm pretty sure that not a single day has passed when I haven't seen at least a few such references. Eventually I got to the point where all the "Twittlering" really bothered me:

> BeckIsALib: If I hear one more stupid, infantile, moronic Hitler analogy, I think I'll scream!!!

Glenn Beck references Hitler quite a bit, perhaps more than any other talk show host out there. A quick Google search for "Glenn Beck" and "Hitler" brings back a rich selection of links.[91] I chose a link to an article from *The Economist* in part because it's not American and in part because the magazine always fills its pages with erudite and comprehensive reporting written in thick prose. I know this because I subscribe to *The Economist* yet rarely manage to read it.

The article in question bears the title "Glenn Beck's Hitler Fetish." In it the author states that "It's kind of fun to write about Mr. Beck, because he's created a zone in which Godwin's Law necessarily ceases to function."

And there's a good example of why I rarely read *The Economist*; deciphering the articles often requires a trip to Wikipedia.

Turns out that Godwin's Law (also known as Godwin's Rule of Nazi Analogies) states that the longer any discussion continues, the greater the odds of some reference to Nazis along the way. Given enough time, every discussion in the universe will eventually include an analogy to the Nazis and/or to Adolph Hitler.

---

[91] In the most harrowing irony yet, just over six million....

It's a brilliant idea, really, and Godwin makes clear that he intends the notion to be only somewhat tongue-in-cheek; he wants us to remember how horrible—truly horrible—Hitler and the Nazis were, and to avoid trite comparisons that only serve to trivialize that horror. Glenn Beck's not paying attention.

Beck's analogies would make Salvador Dali's clock melt. He has compared the Peace Corps to the SS, Obama's health care plan to *Mein Kampf*, and Al Gore's conversations with school kids to recruiting for Hitler's Youth. Dana Milbank, the *Washington Post* writer who first exposed Beck's Hitler obsession in a systematic way (and on whose work *The Economist* piece is partly based) noted that "In his first 18 months on Fox News, from early 2009 through the middle of this year [2010], he [Beck] and his guests invoked Hitler 147 times. Nazis, an additional 202 times. Fascism or fascists, 193 times. The Holocaust got 76 mentions, and Joseph Goebbels got 24."

Thanks to Beck and his compatriots having mainstreamed the idea, it's no surprise that my corner of the Twitterverse runs rampant with Hitlerian references. The far right wing of the GOP considers all Democrats to be Socialists, who are really just Godless Communists in disguise, which makes them Fascists, which makes them Nazis, which makes their leader, President Barack Obama, Hitler. It's the kind of loopy history lesson commonly born from a Glenn Beck chalkboard, with twisted thinking that leads to tweets like these:

JerryRibeye: Liberal Democrat Jews are married to Obama. Hitler was backed by Rothschild, a Jew, some say the king of all Jews.

Getemoutnow: Hitler used radical propaganda and caused the death of 26 million people in WWII. Now Obama is trying to beat that number. He needs to go NOW.

Michael Charney

And this one, from an avowed Glenn Beck superfan who felt compelled to shout his disdain for what he believes are Obama's attempts to mollify the Arab world:

BeckforPrez: HITLER is looking 'UP FROM HELL' and 'PRAISING OBAMA' for his attempt to create a second 'HOLOCAUST' in 'ISRAEL.'

Tweets like these do not merely stretch the analogy, they shred it. These people are referring to a man who introduced a health care plan based on Republican ideas, who wants to raise taxes on the top two percent of income earners, and who has proposed nearly the same Middle East solution as his predecessor George W. Bush, and comparing him to *Adolph Hitler*. How can that possibly make sense to anyone? How can people hold such thoughts in their head and not wonder at their own sanity?

Lest one think that Hitler has a lock on the right, let me disabuse you of that notion. The left are just as prone to Hitlerizing political dialogue. Searching Twitter for the terms "Hitler" and "GOP" turns up tweets like these:

Bizfreak: Backed by the Church, hates minorities & Socialists: What do Hitler and the GOP have in common?

GrinningIndy: If Hitler were alive, being that he was a European white male, the GOP would nominate him.

These constant references to Hitler, absent any irony at all, suggest to me that we've forgotten how good we really have it here in America. Very few of us experienced the Third Reich (including myself), and too many are learning their history from so-called teachers like Beck who layer a fresh ideological coat of whitewash over everything they say. No one needs to care whether Hitlerian hyperbole makes sense because we have nothing to compare it to. We may pretend that having seen *Saving Private Ryan* or *Patton* means that we know what it was like back then, but we really don't. We've never seen anything like the European Theater during World War II. Very few of us have any perspective or any experience with such pain.[92] Our pain these days—the pain that prompts us to compare our president to Adolph Hitler—is the pain of higher gas prices, natural economic cycles, financial and commercial regulations, depressed home values, and potholes. These simplistic and embarrassing comparisons collapse instantly when the scaffold on which they weakly hang is exposed to even the most basic reasoned dialogue.

Nazi analogies are nowhere near as prevalent outside of America. A Twitter search for French President "Sarkozy" and "Hitler," for example, brings up a grand total of one result. Checking for the co-occurrence of Hitler's name with the current German Chancellor Angela Merkel returns just thirteen examples, more than for Sarkozy but still a far cry from the hundreds I found linking The Fuehrer with Barack Obama.

Godwin's law is alive and well and, like much of what we do here in America, we've made it brighter and louder than ever before.

C3   80

In 1994 Glenn Beck wore a ponytail, smoked a lot of pot, and drank himself into regularly scheduled oblivion. He thought about Kurt Cobain and imagined suicide. A rocky marriage and friends

---

[92] For the many who fought for America, both now and then, I know that pain was and is very real. But for the average Joe on the street nothing has ever happened on American soil that compares with what happened to Europe during WWII, at least not since the Civil War.

tired of all the dramatics further contributed to his slide. His zoo-infused radio career required consistently cartoonish behavior; he was fed up with it and felt about as far from his dreams as he could possibly be. His closest friends wore labels and came in fifths. Connecticut, though as close to New York as the proverbial flying crow, was a career away from where he imagined he'd be by this time. And things were not looking up. As Alexander Zaitchik writes, "Alone and peering over the ledge, Beck pulled back. In November of 1994 he attended his first AA meeting. That month he became a dry drunk and stopped smoking weed. He chopped off his ponytail. As 1995 opened, a sober Beck began imagining a future outside of Top 40 radio."

That future would combine a spiritual quest with a concerted study of the talk radio format, and Beck's timing was perfect. Rush Limbaugh ruled the talk radio airwaves, his baritone propelled through countless speakers every day. The Fairness Doctrine, requiring equal time for opposing points of view, had gone the way of the dodo and Clinton-era deregulation now allowed for the conglomeration of hundreds of stations under a single corporate umbrella. These changes—and the rise of a jaded electorate—presaged the perfect storm for right-leaning talk radio. Beck paid attention, listening not only to Rush but also to Bob Grant, an ultra-conservative host who pushed the bounds of good taste from the safe haven of his New York City studio.[93]

With his life turning around and a new-found purpose, Beck refocused on success. The trek back led him to a new marriage (his second wife, Tania), a new religion (Mormonism), and a new career path (political pundit).

---

[93] Actually, that's being kind. I used to listen to Grant when I lived in New Jersey. He was just plain nasty. If you didn't agree with him, he called you names and then slammed down the phone. The man must have learned rhetoric from a third-grader with ADHD.

Hold on. I'm confused. We have Beck at bottom, then climbing back up from the bottom, then every rift heals, and he's ready to conquer the world.

Something in this Meet Glenn Beck story seems too easy, too neat. It reminds me of a newspaper cartoon I once saw in which two scientists are standing in front of a chalkboard filled with a very long and very convoluted calculation. Boldly outlined in the middle of the equation you can see the phrase, "then a miracle occurs." The two scientists are talking; the first is pointing at the chalkboard and saying to the second, "I think you should be more explicit here in step two."

Even Beck's own one-and-a-half page bio sheet provides little more, adding only that he was "faced with divorce from his first wife and separation from his two daughters," and was "emotionally and financially decimated." Considering that Beck openly admits to fourteen years of alcohol and drug abuse and once had a doctor tell him that if he, Beck, didn't sober up he likely wouldn't need to file another year's tax return, I'm inclined to agree with the cartoon scientists. That's biography all tied up in a too-neat bow.

I'd love to think that Beck's story is more than hagiographic myth, but there are simply too many similar biographical tidbits out there—and they all have that same miracle occurring in step two. While the miracle overtones common to recovery are to be expected, Beck's story plays much more dramatically, passing through the doors of his AA meetings and becoming part of his personal mythology, his fairy tale. About.com adds a non-helpful sentence or two by attributing Beck's sobriety to his family "acquainting him with Alcoholics Anonymous." The article on Biography.com isn't much more illuminating, covering this period of his life with, "Beck, trying to make it at a radio station in New Haven, Connecticut, had gone so far as to contemplate suicide before he pulled back and tried to right his life." I'm no expert, but I'm guessing that if you talk to anyone who's been through years of drug and alcohol addiction, they would tell you that it's not quite so simple.

Other biographies provide only slightly more detail. Xander Cricket, in his short (and fawning) book entitled *Glenn Beck: The Redemptive Story of America's Favorite Political Commentator*, treats the resurgence as an actual miracle, attributing Beck's turnaround to the God-given appearance of his future wife, Tania, at the very moment and in the very bar where Beck, standing with his hand wrapped around a Jack and Coke, had decided once and for all to give up the struggle for sobriety.

Sounds like a Lifetime movie script to me.

Dana Milbank, a writer with a bit more pedigree than Xander Cricket, relates pretty much the same story in *Tears of a Clown: Glenn Beck and the Tea Bagging of America*. Beck is drunk, then he's not drunk, then he's possibly going to be drunk again, then Tania-as-miracle appears to cap the tale.

Myths are formed as much from the absence of information as from its presence. We are a story-based species; we feel a compelling need for narrative completion and when we don't have all of the details, we insist on filling them in for ourselves. It doesn't matter that fourteen years of Beck's life earn only a passing biographic nod. There's no need for Beck to disturb the primary crisis-recovery-religion saga, a narrative arc complete enough to serve his message. Beck—and this is brilliant—even folds in his political views as part of the recovery story. In March of 2010 Beck famously announced that he "used to be—believe it or not—a liberal" back before he started attending AA meetings, suggesting that liberalism also requires recovery.

That's some mighty fine storytelling.

Whatever the story's weave, it's clear that once in recovery Beck spent the next few years sitting in a Top-40 seat yet compelled to talk politics, as if his inner voice required expression regardless of the available forum. He often drifted into long rambling conversations with callers who, perplexed by both content and context, simply remained on the line until Beck was done and then politely hung up. This in-between Beck satisfied no one. Not only his audience, but also his management and sponsors were decidedly uncomfortable. It was Scott Shannon, then consulting on morning programs for Clear Channel, who recommended that Beck be given an outlet for his political proclivities. Shannon suggested that Clear Channel allow Beck an additional few hours of air time on one of the network's AM talk radio stations, WELI.

For Beck those few crossover hours served only to tease; he had the talk radio bug. In 1998, convinced more than ever that his career had at last found its proper trajectory, Beck signed with George Hiltzik, a powerful agent who also represented Matt Drudge. Hitzlik's perseverance and phone skills landed Beck some guest slots at what was then (and still is) the pinnacle for talk radio, New York's WABC. After a nervous start Beck found his rhythm, blending chaotic clown with rabid dog, and began to show us ever more solid indications of what was coming.

The view is often better in the rear-view mirror, and looking back at those early days the reasons to worry now seem obvious. Beck disabused one caller of the notion that Jews, Catholics, and Muslims are all the same, then agreed with another that we should be taking the fight to the enemy because, Beck said "war has changed." He quoted—almost verbatim—Sylvester Stallone's closing monologue from *First Blood* and claimed it as the story of an unnamed friend. Truth, fact, and reality became malleable, a pattern he would later turn into an art form as his skills matured and his confidence grew.

Having gotten his first real taste of what a major station could do for him, Beck, with tapes in hand, asked Hiltzik to explore options for full-time talk radio gigs; that effort led Beck to Tampa, where his first eponymous program debuted on January 3, 2000. He went to number one within a year, touching the nerve of an angry conservative constituency in a way that no host previously had. Two years later Beck's show went national, spreading to forty-seven stations, and Beck moved the show's headquarters to Philadelphia. In 2006 Beck landed a regular television gig with CNN, and by 2007 the number of syndicated radio stations broadcasting *The Glenn Beck Program* exceeded 250. He was well on his way to becoming both a good guy and a bad guy—the two kinds of people that Americans most adore.

෭ ෬

Until recently I never quite understood how someone could get sucked into a cult. It made no sense to me that otherwise sane, reasonable, logical, and educated men and women could end up all squirrely, begging on street corners or bowing before a poorly groomed schizophrenic while offering up all of their worldly possessions as preface to yet another in a long string of alien-slash-godhead evolutionary transformations. What Twitter has made me realize, though, is that people don't drape themselves in orange and plant one foot in another dimension right away; that kind of brain-washing takes time.

Reviewing the last few weeks I've noticed that most of my Twittering has veered substantially away from my original target. Lately when I'm in there it's not about Beck at all; instead, most of what I've tweeted has been more like these:

BeckIsALib: Good Lord! Is that Gnewt the Gnome trying to appear centrist? We're in bad shape if he sounds like the rational one!

BeckIsALib: Question: When did Osama become Usama? Is it a media thing so his name doesn't look so much like Obama?

BeckisaLib: Really? John Kerry's the guy we want getting tough with Pakistan? Don't make me laugh.

BeckIsALib: I am still waiting for gas prices to fall... Oil is down a solid 15% in recent weeks. I want my 60¢ drop!

I've slowly become just another @name in the Twittercult, each tweet sent or received another water droplet hitting my forehead until, some 2,500 drops later, I'm different.

I have over 350 followers, a Klout score of fifty-three, a Twitalyzer ranking in the eighty-sixth percentile and membership on nearly two dozen different lists. I'm firing off tweets just to be clever or aggressive. I'm avoiding rudeness not because rudeness bothers me but because I fear a de-following backlash that would make me less influential. I'm engaging with Neo-Nazi's on the right and Robin Hoods on the left. I see words and phrases like "Hitler," "Muslim scumbags," "fascist," and "impeach" every single day, sometimes many, many times. This isn't dialogue. This is just preening and shouting. I feel like I'm in a boiler room full of stock hawkers looking to make a fast buck. That's not what any of this was supposed to be about. I need to take a deep breath and refocus, heal the split between my intentions and my actions.

Put another way, I need to stop embracing my inner jackass.

I spend time thinking about it, about where my own ego sits in this exercise. How do I feel when someone disagrees with me or calls me names? Was I taking it all personally or viewing things objectively? I knew from the beginning that my roles were both actor and observer, but am I keeping the proper balance? I find myself thinking of the famous Stanford prison experiments that I studied in my psych program at Berkeley. Philip Zimbardo, a Stanford professor, designed an experiment in which two dozen students were randomly assigned to take the role of either prisoner or guard in a makeshift prison-lab. All the volunteers knew they were in an experiment, yet within two days the majority of the subjects had completely enrobed themselves in their new roles: "prisoners" showed signs of distress and "guards" showed signs of cruelty. Rebellion broke out among the "prisoners." Zimbardo himself fell into the role of "warden" and had to be reminded by others on the team that he, too, had become part of the experiment. Perhaps most interestingly, not one single volunteer simply asked to leave. All were so enmeshed in their roles that they had forgotten that they still had their freedom.

Here I am, prisoner, guard, and warden in my own experiment. It's time to remind myself what I'm doing, why I'm doing it and—importantly—who's in charge:

> BeckIsALib: I seem to have lost focus, so am going back to proving that Beck is a liberal actor, not a conservative at all, but a traitor.

Hitting the send button felt like rinsing the dust off of my skin after a sandstorm. I then put together a barrage of Beck-related tweets, pulling no punches: everything was about Beck being a phony, an actor, and a general all-around hypocrite:

> BeckIsALib: #GlennBeck said "The poorest are being hit by inflation harder than anybody else."

> BeckIsALib: According to a New York Times story, #GlennBeck has betrayed his conservative Christian base.

> BeckIsALib: O'Reilly starts distancing himself from #GlennBeck. Perhaps he's starting to see Beck for the actor that he really is.

BeckIsALib: #GlennBeck admits he's a comedian: It's about time.

In total, nineteen tweets launched in under ten seconds[94], virtually guaranteeing that my @name and logo would commandeer a chunk of real estate on all those other timelines.

The barrage worked. A flurry of activity arrived within minutes and the topic of Beck's credibility took center stage. Some tweets were dismissive, others curious. One tweeter in particular cogently challenged my decidedly eleventh-grade approach:

MrSkeptic: @BeckIsALib Do you source any of your claims so people can validate them?

BeckIsALib: @MrSkeptic Yep; let me know which ones you're interested in; I've got citations.

I tweeted the links but never heard back. I'm guessing that @MrSkeptic took one look at them and decided that he didn't agree with my conclusions.

Others were more willing to converse. @SouthernandCross, very right and very smart, noting my tweet about Beck wanting to save our remaining resources...

BeckIsALib: #GlennBeck said "We should save the resources that we have left."

...came back with this tweet:

---

[94] Using a Twitter scheduling tool, naturally.

SouthernandCross: As if we're squandering them now...What a fraud!

She in turn found herself challenged by another tweeter, @Texastea56, who pointed out that I had sourced my information from the incredibly liberal *MediaMatters* website.

Texastea56 @SouthernandCross: Ma'am, you're retweeting Media Matters. I wouldn't believe anything that comes from them. They twist and warp everything.

Still, @SouthernandCross—a self-proclaimed member of the Tea Party—defended me, suggesting that perhaps Glenn Beck wasn't all sunshine and daisies:

Southernandcross @Texastea56: You don't have to be Media Matters to find a lot wrong with what Beck says.

They went back and forth a few more times; I stayed out of it to see what would happen. Gratifyingly, the idea that Glenn Beck might have feet of clay caromed back and forth without my adding any more to the conversation. There were people out there—people on the right—who thought a bit like I did.

I felt like I'd just been given a new puppy.

CB ΣΟ

Newt's in; Huck and the Donald are out. The Twitterverse yawns.

On Saturday Mike Huckabee used his own Fox News show to non-announce. He teased his audience during the day's promos and the show's opening monologue, and then made them sit through the usual mix of pontification and guest rants. Then, in a scene that played like an audition for a remake of *This is Spinal Tap*, Huck strapped on his custom Overture bass (christened the "Huck Bass") and joined the insanely talented Ted Nugent on stage where they both cranked it up to eleven. Frustrated yet again by the way entertainment and politics constantly merge, I fired off this tweet:

BeckIsALib: So, did #Huckabee decide he's going to the Miami Heat? Oh, wait...different circus.

Finally, as the show closed, Mike told us that his "heart said no" and that he would therefore not join the race for the 2012 nomination. Casting his decision as spiritual, Huckabee added that:

"I don't expect everyone to understand this, but I am a believer and a follower of Jesus Christ and that relationship is far more important to me than any political office. For me, the discussion and decision is not a political one, not a financial one. It's not even a practical one. It's a spiritual one."

The news landed with an anticlimactic thud but did spawn at least a few clever tweets:

ArkansasMom12: Breaking News..... God whispered into Huckabee's ear to keep on doing his crappy show.

RetaketheWH: Huckabee: "My Heart Says No;" I think his wallet was threatening to beat the crap out of his heart!!

Huckabee's one-act play generated the expected spike in tweet traffic but somehow it all felt watered down; people were tweeting just to tweet. I felt that way, too, like I had an obligation to say something. My only real motivation was the desire to appear clever, but unfortunately I'd already peaked with the LeBron James reference. I lobbed a few more out there, but my heart just wasn't in it.

Huck's decision also triggered tweets from the hopelessly optimistic, those still married to candidates whose prospects have roughly the same life expectancy as a Snickers bar in a roomful of five-year-olds:

> DogLover89: Huckabee's out. Palin angered the Fox News Gods. Pawlenty's a stiff. Romney's a Dem. This thing is Trump's to lose.

I somehow doubt that, @DogLover89, especially since your guy isn't in it anymore, either.

By the middle of the week Trump decided that he'd had his fun with the press and the Prez, and that he wasn't really all that interested in such a low-paying job. It's unfortunate; I and many others will miss the spectacle. Hell, we haven't even seen any of Obama's birthmarks yet.

It will be interesting to see what Beck says about all this; he's never been a fan of Trump and he and Huckabee have been feuding of late, with Beck recently calling Huckabee thin-skinned, and—even worse—a progressive. Huckabee didn't take it well, suggesting that Beck needed to "clean his gun and point it more carefully lest it blow up in his face."

With Huckabee gone, the GOP has a gap to fill in the ultra-conservative slot. I fully expected the right wing radio rodeo to start pushing names, and I wasn't disappointed. Many bandied about Michele Bachmann's *bona fides*, and Herman Cain upped his PR machine in order to silence the quiet. Both Pawlenty and Santorum kept reminding the base of their own solidly conservative credentials, but neither is making any noise in the polls and the Tea Party vote still seems up for grabs. Calls continue, of course, for Sarah Palin.

Through it all Glenn Beck remained topically silent. Turns out he's way too distracted by his latest shiny new toy: Israel.

Beck identifies himself as a long-time supporter of Israel and, while Beck has had occasional forays into fringe anti-Jewish conspiracy theories (such as *The Protocols of the Learned Elders of Zion*, a fraudulent text published in Russia near the turn of the last century and purporting to be a Jewish plan for total world domination), those missteps have more to do with Beck's loosely-bound chalkboard history than any blatant anti-Semitism. There's no reason not to take him at his word on this one. He has often spoken out in Israel's defense; back in 2010, after Israel boarded an IHH ship ostensibly on a humanitarian mission and took a licking in the press because of the raid, Beck claimed that Israel was "once again the world's target." More recently, in March 2011, he used his television show's opening segment to remind us to "take a stand for Israel." He has never believed in Obama's Middle East policies and sees any concession to the Arab or Muslim worlds as another step in a slippery-sloped conspiracy inevitably targeting Israel's demise and the emergence of a modern-day Caliphate.[95]

Glenn Beck never does anything halfway. After years of discussing Israel on radio, television, and in print, he finally took his show on the road, heading over to Israel for a few meet-and-greets, some hummus and tahini, and a chance to cry at the Wailing Wall. He also made a few speeches reminding everyone that he supported Israel even if America's president didn't. He then came home.

Immediately upon his return Beck announced that he'd be heading back later this summer, this time to lead a rally in Jerusalem. The rally, he says, aims to "restore courage."

---

[95] Interestingly, the small but vocal ultra-right wing has long been the locus for anti-Semitic fringe groups but has shifted strongly to a pro-Israel stance since 9/11. "The Jew is the perfect anti-Islamist," writes Jonathan Kay in *Among the Truthers*. "America's fight is Israel's fight...Support for Israel has remained one of the few issues to attract virtually unanimous bipartisan support."

"Glenn is looking for people around the world to find their own personal courage," his website tells us, and for just five grand or so you can join the pilgrimage and stand shoulder to shoulder with our Israeli brethren. Seems a bit silly to me. I can't imagine that Israelis have much interest in restoring courage: they've never lost it.

It's great publicity, though, and right about now Beck can use it. Now that his "discussions" with Fox are safely in the rear-view mirror his biggest risk is invisibility; Glenn Beck feeds on the public eye and since Israel and the Middle East are topics that are both important and emotional, any activity in that region—even activity by Beck—is pretty much guaranteed press coverage. Beck got his.

Press coverage inevitably leads to Twittered reactions, of course, with the usual suspects spitting out hundreds of polarized comments:

Jondoneit: Glenn Beck stands up for Israel, Obama bows to Muslim dictators. I choose Beck.

Julie4198: Glenn Beck's Absurd Jerusalem Rally: Why are religious conservatives obsessed with Israel?

One tweep linked to an article intimating that Beck is all about the money. The last line of the article reads "For Beck, what's really important is his 40 million dollar annual take and fledgling media empire. Forbes just ranked the former rodeo clown as its thirtieth most powerful celebrity."

BusdriverRalph: The last line says all! He's in it for the $! Beck's Absurd Jerusalem Rally.

Watch your wallets, pilgrims.

I wondered if these responses—mostly from the U.S.—were indicative of how those in Israel felt about Glenn Beck dancing the hora all over their culture. I'm fortunate to know quite a few people in Israel and, coincidentally, I had just hung up the phone after talking with one of them, a woman named Michal with whom I had worked for a number of years. She is one of many friends I have there; for several years I managed an international team of software developers for Thomson Reuters and the bulk of my staff worked in an office park just outside of Tel Aviv. I've been to Israel perhaps two dozen times in the last few years.

Michal, for whom I acted as manager and mentor earlier in her career and who has now successfully risen to a position of significant responsibility, wanted my advice regarding a management team meeting she had scheduled for the upcoming week. Prior to getting into her questions, however, I preempted her agenda just long enough to ask what she thought of Beck and his recent visit to Israel.

"Who?"

"Glenn Beck. He was just in Israel. I'm wondering what Israelis thought of his visit."

"I didn't get the name. Who was it who was here?"

Perhaps we were fighting a garbled Skype connection. I tried again.

"Glenn. Beck. He's a right-wing radio personality here in the U.S. He's just come back from Israel. Supposedly it was a big deal. I think he's planning on going back in August to have some kind of rally for courage or something."

"Never heard of him. I can ask around, but I don't think anyone else has, either."

Interesting.

"I do know who Anderson Cooper is, though," Michal said. "I was in New York a few months ago and I ran into him on the street. I recognized him right away."

Hmmm. Glenn, you might want to take note. It seems that Israel has other things to do than think about you.

WEEK TEN:
MANIFESTO DESTINY

I
t just doesn't seem fair. All week it's been wet and dreary and tomorrow the End Times are coming. You'd think that if God were truly planning horror and mayhem for those Left Behind, He could at least have scheduled some nice weather before going all four horsemen on our asses.

I'm not really that worried, though. Harold Camping, president of Family Radio and predictor of the May 21, 2011 Rapture, doesn't have the greatest track record. He predicted the Rapture once before in 1994; he even wrote a book about it. When that prediction deflated, Camping told us that he had misread the Biblical code used to calculate the date. I'm guessing he'll say something similar this time. Checking the virtual pulse tells me that everyone agrees with me; hell, even Vegas won't give odds on this one.

This time Camping aims for precision: he's provided the exact five-month window during which the End Times will ravage the earth, with the actual, physical, cataclysmic, and absolutely final End of the World scheduled for October 21, 2011. Again it doesn't seem fair. God should hold off for a couple of weeks and maybe let the

Cubbies win the World Series, just out of respect for the people who have been praying for it all these years.

It's been fun in Twitterville as the hour winds closer and the world winds down. My timeline looks like it's been taken over by school kids during recess, everyone sprinting back and forth across the playground like they've just been unchained from their desks. One tweep, @Judgmentornot, opens up a thread that invites others to exercise their wit:

Judgmentornot: Judgment Day Open Thread: How are you planning to celebrate The Rapture on May 21?

The tweet links to a website where people respond quickly and frequently:

Rickysplain: I will, of course, be joining the roughly 600,000 people engaging in post-rapture looting.

Scienceguy: I'll be doing research. A lot of cars will be unmanned come the rapture, and I want to see if God is truly a skilled co-pilot.

Wickedsense: My cousin John says that he's buying up a bunch of blow-up sex dolls, filling them with helium and releasing them to heaven.

This last suggestion, both witty and obscure, references an episode of *Six Feet Under*, the HBO series about a family-run funeral home that opened each episode with someone dying. In one particular show—entitled "In Case of Rapture"—a woman driving along a city street sees inflated sex dolls floating in the sky off in the distance and, thinking it's the Rapture, jumps out of her car and runs headlong into traffic. Or maybe @Wickedsense just wants to make sure that the Raptured don't have to do without certain earthly pleasures. If so, I admire his compassion.

One gentleman who owns his own photography studio is running a twenty-one-percent Rapture Special (in celebration of the apocalyptic date, one assumes). Another tweeter, @BearMountain, posted a "Will You Be Raptured?" flowchart, quite useful if you're not sure whether you should make plans for next week. Turns out that anyone who's ever taken the Lord's name in vain, or has ever stolen anything, or has ever wanted more money or a bigger house, or has ever eaten pork or shellfish or reptile or rodent or camel, or has ever worn wool or linen, is in big trouble. I haven't done the math but I figure that leaves a Rapture-Ready population of maybe eight people, a couple of whom might not even be Christians. On a positive note, if Harold Camping can prove that a mere eight people have gone missing, then he can claim prescience and die a happy man.

Other parts of the world seem even less concerned than we are. The British, for example, are blithely (yet politely) ignoring the matter altogether:

TheBritishMonarchy: On 21 May: The Prince of Wales - Patron, Music in Country Churches, will attend a concert at St. Mary.

Team_Barrowman: John Barrowman News—John Barrowman to be guest judge on So You Think You Can Dance BBC1 21 May.[96]

I've seen precisely zero tweets from anyone who believes that the Rapture will actually happen tomorrow. That's not to say that there

---

[96] John Barrowman is the Scottish-born and Illinois-raised actor best known for playing Captain Jack Harkness on the BBC (and now Starz) series *Torchwood*. He's sort of a cross between a young Harry Hamlin and King Julien, the ring-tailed lemur from *Madagascar*. The Prince of Wales is the Prince of Wales.

aren't plenty of people who believe that the Rapture will happen someday, just not right now.[97]

We can make fun of Camping all we want but he's a product of his time, a period in history when everything we deem important requires declaration. We no longer just talk to each other; we can't hear ourselves through the noise. We have to rise above so we shout, scream, exaggerate, magnify, overstate, embellish, and embroider. We publish, blog, post, and tweet, doing whatever it takes to be heard. We turn our beliefs into worldviews, our worldviews into declarations and our declarations into manifestos, each one more bombastic that the last, hoping that, eventually, we'll get one of them right or, failing that, at least get others to believe that it's right.

❈ ❈

"Manifesto" is one of those words that literary types refer to as having weight, which means that we can't even utter the word without triggering emotional responses steeped in prejudice, history and culture. There are many such words in our language, from simple and obvious words like "black" and "white" to more subtle words like "value" and "educated." Many of these weighted words, not surprisingly, have become politicized; just about anything with visceral resonance does, eventually.[98]

Thanks mostly to Karl Marx the word "manifesto" is now tightly bound to our concepts of communism, socialism, and totalitarianism. These are bad things, connected historically to those who want to kill

---

[97] I find this a curious disconnect. If the belief is truly deep-seated, then why not right now? Why don't believers live every day like the Rapture is tomorrow?

[98] Which makes me wonder whether we shouldn't put certain emotion-dulling drugs in the Congressional drinking water. Something like Diazepam might work but the risk is that Congress might move even slower than it does now.

us, torture us, breed with our women, smash our churches, brainwash our children, and take *A Prairie Home Companion* off the air. Communism, socialism, and totalitarianism are evil; communists, socialists, and totalitarians are the bad guys. Once it was the Soviet Union and North Vietnam; now it's China and North Korea. It doesn't matter: for many people it's the classic threat based on the classic manifesto.

Other twentieth-century manifestos reinforce the fear. *Mein Kampf* gives us almost the same shiver as Marx's *Manifesto of the Communist Party*. The Unabomber, Ted Kaczynski, wrote a manifesto (actually entitled *Industrial Society and its Future*), endless pages of rambling neo-Luddite scree that were eventually printed, under demand, by both *The New York Times* and *The Washington Post*.[99] All of these now imprint our cultural psyches, bad things written by bad people, and I'll bet a money-filled briefcase that the next crazy with world-changing aspirations will have a manifesto, too.

Most manifestos aren't negative. Philosophers, scientists, and writers pen manifestos and use the word as originally defined: a public declaration of principle and intention. *The Russell-Einstein Manifesto* of 1955 (issued by philosopher Bertrand Russell and famously co-signed by Albert Einstein) highlighted the dangers of nuclear war. Philosopher Donna Haraway's *Cyborg Manifesto* delineates a new notion of feminism (which she deemed Cyborg Theory). Even Mozilla, the famous no-one-owns-the-internet collective, has a manifesto, uncreatively named the *Mozilla Manifesto*, which outlines the key beliefs and principles of the Mozilla project as "a global community of people who believe that openness, innovation, and opportunity are key to the continued health of the internet." There's even a *Cannibal Manifesto*, written by Brazilian poet Oswald de Andrade in 1928. Unfortunately, it turns out not to be what I was

---

[99] *Penthouse* offered to publish it first, but Ted thought it inappropriate.

hoping for when I spotted the title, but is instead a series of brief statements supporting Brazil's history of cannibalizing other cultures. It includes gems like "Only Cannibalism unites us. Socially. Economically. Philosophically." and "We had the right codification of vengeance. The codified science of Magic. Cannibalism. For the permanent transformation of taboo into totem." Frankly, Oswald, all of that seems meaningless to me. Something about zombies and necrophilia would have been far more interesting.

This morning I launched a tweet asking what people think about the word "manifesto." I figured that the political junkies with whom I regularly communicate might find the topic interesting:

BeckIsALib: Research question: When you hear the word "manifesto," what immediately pops into your head? Please RT; collecting info. Thanks.

The first response came back in just a couple of minutes. It was a link to a porn site.

After several hours of silence, I fired off the same tweet again. Perhaps a different time of day would attract a different group of people. Again I received nothing in return. I was (and am) disappointed that not one single person of the several hundred who follow me thought it worth the time to answer my question. I'll just have to stick with my own opinions on this one.[100]

Manifestos should be declarations about what we want, about what our dreams are, and about how we see those dreams coming true. They should be both large and small, both personal and global, both internal and external. They should represent ourselves as we are, as others see us, and as we want to be seen. They should be full of big ideas and small actions, sweeping generalizations, and indi-

---

[100] That shouldn't be hard. I've already decided what I believe.

vidual details, a collection of principled principles and, above all, should be written with weeping sincerity.

It's also best if they don't sound like they've been drafted in a backwoods cabin by someone who weaves birdseed into his beard and cuts his toenails with a dulled machete.

ɔʒ ʚ

Both the Democratic and Republican parties have manifestos, though I doubt either would willingly admit it. They certainly don't use the word publicly. A search on Twitter for the words "Manifesto" and "Republican" returns only one sarcastic tweet. Note the hash tag:

NotAChance2012: The Republican Manifesto
#lessinterestingbooks

The same search for "Manifesto" and "Democrat" returns only one link as well, this one for a political party in Scotland.

The Democratic manifesto requires allegiance to a set of beliefs based on the self-evident need for a government-sponsored, government-provided, cradle-to-grave safety net.[101] Democrats want us all to believe that everyone's welfare is everyone's responsibility, that it's possible (and wrong) to have too much of something, that many people are entitled to assistance and should take it even if they don't want it or need it, that big business is bent on consolidating wealth and power in the hands of the few, and that the overall needs of the many are more important (and ultimately more valuable) than those

---

[101] There's plenty of justification for this, by the way. People are notoriously prone to instant gratification at the expense of their own future, and then whining about it later on when things tighten up and some benevolent overseer (whether parent, school, or government) won't step in and help out. Ditto for corporations.

of the individual. It also helps if you have just a little bit of unadmitted prejudice for those who haven't attained a college degree or read anything by Dostoevsky.

The left's unwritten manifesto at least attempts inclusivity. The Democrat comes from anywhere and everywhere: poor and rich, white and black, east and west. The Republican manifesto, in contrast, acts as gatekeeper, litmus test, and all-around vetting machine, St. Peter at the Pearlies passing judgment on a long line of aspirants. It's a rigid, get-in-line approach to manifesto—and the line is always on the right. Anyone who doesn't abide by the party principles can expect a rapid trip to the woodshed. Candidates, in particular, have a tough time of it; any that refuse to abide by the manifesto's unwritten principles have very little chance of winning the nomination.

First, you must accept that taxes are bad and spending cuts are good, ignoring the obvious triteness of this Aristotelian statement. There is no middle ground, no situation under which additional taxes on some people might make sense. Second, America and its populace are blessed by God; we are the greatest country in the history of mankind and our way of life is almost (if not totally) perfect. Any attempts to prove otherwise (with facts, for example) is simply unpatriotic. Third, there is nothing—nothing—laudable that a Democrat can do because Democrats are the "liberal elite" parading around with slightly lifted noses and talking down to the common man while trying to take everyone's money and give it to *them*. Fourth, there is always a *them*. Finally, the manifesto requires that any viable candidate unequivocally support any and all positions promoted by the religious right wing of the party, including the absolute wrongness of abortion, the absolute rightness of bearing arms, the absolute certainty of Christian principles, and the absolute blind obedience to the loudest voice in the room.[102]

---

[102] It also helps if you fawningly admire all of the rewritten American history used to support these views.

Bottom line: to gain the Democratic nomination you have to pretend that you care about everyone whether you do or not, but if you want the GOP nomination you may very well need to check your soul at the door.

The latest Republican choosing to abandon his self-respect is Jon Huntsman, a name I've just heard for the first time. Apparently he is or was the governor of Utah and is or was the United States ambassador to China. He has said both nice and not-so-nice things about President Obama. *The Economist* likes him. Widely considered a moderate Republican, Huntsman has recently reversed a number of his previous positions on several issues including health care, carbon emissions, and the value of federal stimulus during a recession.

Huntsman has apparently read the GOP's manifesto and determined his hypocrisy thusly. I can only assume that means he plans a run for the nomination.

CR   BO

Sometimes political thinking produces an effect very similar to an out-of-body-experience, allowing a person to look at themselves both subjectively and objectively at the same time. I'm very aware, for example, that my impressions of the two parties emerge largely from the stereotypes I've internalized over the years. Yet at the same time I realize that I'm still carry those stereotypes around with me. Sometimes it feels like I'm wearing a fanny pack that I hope no one notices. I guess that makes me a hypocrite, too.

My own political biography could probably fit on the back of a napkin. It wouldn't even have to be a full-size napkin. I'd just need something small, like the ones they give out at Dunkin' Donuts with the Munchkins. Though I knew when I started this experiment that I would be talking politics, I can't say that I had any desire to entangle myself in any real political dialogue. I just assumed I could play around the edges, collect a few outrageous and oddball tweets to flavor my writing, and then move on. Naively I believed that I was not one of *those* people; I was the sociological observer while they were the experimental subjects. I would play the role of Philip Zimbardo in this exercise but would resist the urge to become part of it myself.

I began with all my prejudices in place. On one side I expected mostly nutjobs and whackos sitting at home and ignorantly blathering on and on while polishing their guns and fish logos. On the other side I expected mostly literati and logicians conversing with other elevated noses while listening with half an ear to *All Things Considered* and preparing an early-evening cocktail drizzled with St. Germain elderflower liqueur. I had read the manifestos, too, it seemed, and as a result I knew exactly who these people were.

Only they weren't.

We are all of us prejudiced. We float in a sea of stereotypes like a fish in water: we are so immersed in it, it is so a part of our world, that we don't even know it's there; we don't even know what it means to be wet.[103]

I share these same prejudices and have all my life. I grew up in a predominately white, Jewish neighborhood, Hancock Park, in Los Angeles. Recently a classmate from that time invited me to join a Facebook group where she had gathered photos and comments from the Hancock Park class of 1969. She had—God bless her—saved every class photo from that time, some in faded colors and others in grainy black and white, but all in remarkable condition considering

---

[103] I'm not the first to use this analogy, and certainly won't be the last. Nobel Prize winner Mario Vargas Llosa titled his 1993 memoir *A Fish in the Water (El Pez en el Agua)*. My favorite, though, is David Foster Wallace's brilliant *This is Water: Some Thoughts, Delivered on a Significant Occasion, about Living a Compassionate Life*. The book, a commencement address that Wallace gave at Kenyon College in 2005, is all the more poignant for having been published after the author's depression-induced suicide in 2008.

that they had probably languished for forty years or more at the bottom of some memorabilia-filled cardboard box.

In looking at the pictures the first thing I noticed was the disconnect between what I thought of myself then (what we all must have thought of ourselves then) and the locked-in-time faces staring into a long-ago camera. We were small. And we dressed funny. There was Roberta in the front row wearing a cross between a sailor suit and a Catholic school girl's uniform. Julia, standing next to her, wore a dress so yellow that today, even faded, the color reminds me of Blue Bonnet margarine. Next to Julia is Henry, wearing a cross between an ascot and a bolo.

I'm in the third row back, just in front of Margaret and wearing a bright orange shirt that is exactly the same color as Margaret's dress. If you glance quickly at the picture you might be fooled into thinking that her head is growing out of my shoulder in some sick, Zaphod Beebelbrox[104] sort of way. Mrs. Jemmond, our teacher, stands to the left of the class; she isn't smiling, consistent with how I remember her: incredibly tough but incredibly fair. (When anyone asks me who my favorite teacher was from back then Mrs. Jemmond is never on the list. But when someone asks me about my best teachers over the years, hers is always the first name I think of.) There were other pictures in the collection, too, including one of Mrs. Guidry's sixth-graders (the other half of our graduating class). Different faces stood in similar rows.

The membership in the Facebook group slowly grew as each of us added friends we noticed in the pictures: I added Jerry; Lisa added Ruth and Jim. Four or five of us began exchanging messages about

---

[104] The two-headed Galactic President (temporary) from *The Hitchhiker's Guide to the Galaxy* (as opposed to the Ottawa, Canada nightclub). Zaphod is one of my personal heroes, mostly because the second head rarely speaks but when it does it manages to sound both intelligent and useless at the same time, spitting out quotes like, "Quiet. We're thinking." That's real talent.

the pictures, mostly trying to remember the names that went with the faces. Forty-two years is a long time. Is that Jill in the middle row, or Angela? Did Richard spell his last name with a "J" or a "G?" Wow...is that Debra? I don't even remember her from back then....

Two days later we had identified perhaps eighty percent of the kids in those class photos. We shared a few virtual high-fives in recognition of both teamwork and memory. There was one major gap, though: we had identified only a few of the dozen or more non-white classmates. Of those, I had recognized a couple of almost-familiar faces but could name none. I felt immediately guilty about it.

That makes me prejudiced. Not the forgetting. The feeling guilty.

In part I felt guilty because I believed I was supposed to. I didn't first take a moment to think about how those kids hadn't lived in my neighborhood, nor did I consider all the white faces I had failed to identify. I only thought about the obvious facts: I was white, the kids I knew were white, and the kids I didn't know were not.

None of this makes me a bigot, though. Having prejudices and being a bigot are loosely related but are not the same thing. We all have prejudices; whether we embrace them or fight them defines our bigotry.

Bigotry travels down two roads. The first welcomes those who cling to their prejudices, never even trying to overcome them. Many aren't even aware of their own beliefs, worn like tattoos so old they've become just another part of their skin. Others don their big-otry like medieval armor blood-stained after a long and exhausting battle. Such bigotry comes in all skin colors and religions, and spouts all manner of creed and manifesto.

The second road invites those who are so self-righteous, who try so hard not to exhibit any prejudice, that the resulting behaviors scream out their discriminations.

I remember watching *All in the Family* back in the early seventies when it was still shockingly new. I laughed when Archie Bunker lashed out at kikes and spics and jungle bunnies because it was so obvious that he was the intended target of ridicule.[105] But when his son-in-law Mike spoke, I cringed. Mike's over-the-top righteousness made him the blind one in the family, not Archie. He was so convinced he was right, so argumentative, so apparently inclusive yet blatantly dismissive at the same time. He refused to see how his own prejudices shaped his behavior, and this blindness made him even more of a bigot than his father-in-law. This second kind of bigotry, combined as it is with hypocrisy, is much worse. Michael Stivic really was a meathead.

I expected to find a great deal of first-order bigotry out there in the Twitterverse and I was not disappointed, but where I found it surprised me. My own prejudice planned for it on the far right, but I found it as well on the far left. From the right one can find things like this:

RightnotLeft: Whenever I see a towelhead in the airport, I automatically think they are terrorists.

The left—and, as I said, I certainly didn't expect this—can be just as abrupt:

IsWhatItIs: It's good to see someone calling a spade a spade— "Herman Cain Is A 'Religious Bigot' For Comments about Muslims."

Herman Cain, you may recall, is an African American. I don't believe for a moment that @IsWhatItIs chose his words carelessly.

Extremists comfortably reside at both ends of the political spectrum, and many spend their tweeting time screaming at each

---

[105] Quick: how many of you just winced reading those words?

other in vulgar, bigoted language. Every racist rant from the right is soon counterpunched with an equally horrific outburst from the left. Language flies. Creative name calling crashes down from the atmosphere. Parents: lock up your children.

The unexpected bigotry on the far left, laced as it is with the blindness and hypocrisy of a thousand Michael Stivics, frightens me much more than what I found on the right. The left is where I find tweeps who want to "protect" those who have never asked for protection, who want to fix attitudes, and who want to correct the words that others use to make them less offensive yet don't even recognize the irony of such attempts. People in this latter category are frightening because they're close-minded in their open-mindedness, a dangerous oxymoron that leads some to think they're better than everyone else. It also frightens me that so many have so casually embraced the conventional wisdom[106] that liberalism precludes prejudice yet conservatism defines it; that's just another marketing message too easily absorbed and mythologized.

We build myth from these bigotries and hypocrisies—small stories about what we "know" to be right or wrong, fair or unfair, moral or immoral—and from these myths we build manifestos large and small. The small, sometimes personal, manifestos are individual and subtle, undoubtedly arising one sentence at a time until a sentence becomes a page, a page becomes a chapter, a chapter becomes a book, a way of living. We then take this way of living and send it, like Voyager into the universe, 140 characters at a time, hoping someone sees it, reads it, and believes it, too.

---

[106] For a nice take on conventional wisdom, check out "Mark's Daily Apple" at http://www.marksdailyapple.com/the-definitive-guide-to-conventional-wisdom/. I particularly like how he describes conventional wisdom as "a lumbering beast: slow to move, but difficult to alter course once its big bullish head is set on moving in a certain direction. It's the pigheaded, stubborn curmudgeon yelling at those darn kids to get off his lawn."

Cʒ ꙮ

Myths become powerful tools for those who would manipulate us. Given as we are to seeking patterns and building stories, a carefully worked myth quickly worms its way into our collective conscience; a meme planted over a very short period quickly and virally spirals into the minds of many. The key to creating these myths, to having us believe them and then serving as their couriers, is marketing. Simple, basic marketing. Our attachment to social issues is no different than our attachment to Coke or Pepsi, to Crest or Colgate, except as a matter of degree. Marketers work to create a message that creates an emotional bond and when they find it, they pound it into our skulls over and over again. A health care program becomes "Obamacare." The wealthiest Americans become "Job Creators." The Republicans become "The Party of 'No'." Ronald Reagan becomes "The Great Communicator." Political groups come together periodically to plan their talking points and sometimes even hire outside firms to help create messages they believe will resonate with the relevant constituencies. These messages, once born, are incubated by the pundits and talking heads, repeated endlessly by Rush, Glenn, Rachel, Joe, Chris, Sean, and Alan until the words emerge, matured and ready for use by those on either side who share the beliefs of those they listen to. The phrases are catchy, clever, and always—always—short enough to fit in a tweet. The myth explodes across a rapidly moving virtual landscape until it soon becomes truth.

Perhaps no myth has so polluted the current political dialogue as the one that now has complete control over the Republican Party: the Myth of Reagan. This myth is an extensive rewrite of our fortieth president, rebroadcast daily on talk radio, talk television, and throughout the Twittersphere.[107] So much has been recast regarding

---

[107] In a moment of irony that could easily make a David Letterman Top Ten list, the Democratic party has now taken to invoking Reagan as well, likening him to a great

both the man and his legacy that the original person is largely invisible today, eclipsed by an iconic shadow even he could never have imagined would loom quite so broadly across the modern political landscape.[108]

Ronald Reagan was not a terribly conservative man either personally or professionally. He voted for Franklin Delano Roosevelt four times and supported both Harry Truman in 1948 and George McGovern in his 1960 run for the Minnesota Senate. As governor of California—long known as one of the country's most liberal states—he signed the Therapeutic Abortion Act that ensured that abortions in California would only be performed by licensed medical practitioners working in clean, safe clinics. Reagan also signed the Family Law Act (which allowed no-fault claims from either party), thereby making it easier for California couples to divorce.

As governor, Reagan was certainly to the right of center on social issues, but not that far right. While he routinely lambasted the "bums" on welfare and the "mess" at Berkeley, his actions rarely matched his rhetoric. Rhetoric, however, gets voters to the polls, a truism Reagan understood and a lesson since absorbed by the social conservatives in the GOP. Rhetoric helps win elections, after which the elected can govern as they originally intended.

Reagan's presidency differed little from his governorship, with his words leaning more heavily right than his actions. While he

---

compromiser (he was) and a president who raised taxes when he had to (he did). Still, even the truth seems unpalatable when blatantly politicized. I imagine Dianne Feinstein biting her tongue every time she hears the analogy and then wondering, during some sleepless night, why she didn't just become a cable-car conductor.

[108] Just to prove I'm not a total jackass, I'm going to admit to another of the very few times when I admire Glenn Beck. While the man has promoted some of the most egregious mythical rewrites of our day, he has always been highly skeptical of any myths about our recent presidents, including both Ronald Reagan and George Bush II. His not-so-terrible book, *Broke*, covers these issues in some detail.

appointed one very conservative Supreme Court justice in Antonin Scalia, he also seated two moderate justices, Sandra Day O'Connor and Anthony Kennedy. On the subject of abortion he was somewhat vocal but legislatively silent, nor was he one to regularly attend church services despite his claim to be "born again."

The mythmakers have rewritten that entire legacy, turning the rhetoric into truth and ignoring the facts. Supreme Court appointments often turn out differently than intended. California is so liberal he had no choice. Going to church would have put others at risk.[109] Many political figures begin as liberals but eventually mature. These justifications abound, endlessly etched into "history," sold as marketing sound bites, and then regurgitated as manifesto.[110]

Even more ironic is the fact that Reagan never exercised the fiscal conservatism that now lies at the heart of the modern Republican rubric. He based his policies on a new and unproven set of theories which came to be known as supply-side economics (or "trickle-down" economics to its detractors). The underlying principle of supply-side theory was to count on low taxes creating the wealth that would create the jobs that would generate more tax revenue, even at these ultimately lower tax rates. Betting on such a theory meant that Reagan could safely grow his government to an unprecedented size (which he did) while betting on the revenue growth from an energized economy. The policy added substantially to the federal deficit when the expected revenue growth failed to materialize.

---

[109] I see this claim frequently, but it doesn't explain why Reagan rarely attended church prior to his entry into political life nor why Bill and Hillary Clinton managed to go to church quite calmly through most of their incumbency.

[110] But let's not paint Reagan as a liberal; he wasn't. He cut social programs in favor of increased defense spending, was no friend to public unions, and was less carrot than stick on foreign policy matters. He was right of center. But the center was still in the center back then and by today's standards Reagan was probably left of even John McCain on most social and economic issues.

Today's newly minted "Reagan Conservative" is pure myth, a fiction that has replaced facts with what conservatives claim they "know" about Reagan. Frankly, I doubt that the real Ronald Reagan could even win his party's nomination in today's climate; he would likely be classed as a Republican In Name Only—a RINO—the latest insult dividing the Tea Party from the (former) Republican mainstream.[111]

On any given day one can see the Myth of Reagan perpetuated constantly in the Twitterverse, as in this conversation I had with @Truegop432, whose opening salvo discredited Chris Christie, the current governor of New Jersey, as yet one more antiquated, out-of-touch RINO.

> Truegop432: Can someone explain to me why Conservatives are so gung-ho for Christie? He's a RINO. Who cares how tough he acts in a press conference?

I don't often take offense at name calling, but the term RINO raises my hackles. Using the term is akin to saying that 150 years of Republican beliefs (including those of Abraham Lincoln) were phony and that only since Ronald Reagan (myth-made version) has the true and conservative Republican Party emerged. When I see that myth spat out into the Twittersphere, I get cranky. I had to respond.

> BeckIsALib: @Truegop432 I'm always compelled to shout out against the term RINO. It's rude; the best GOP presidents have always been moderate, including Reagan.

---

[111] If you think my assertion pure flummery, try to imagine all those "Reagan Democrats" voting for Sarah Palin or Mike Huckabee. Do people really think those moderates crossed over because Reagan was so radically conservative?

From there things just got worse. I had attacked the conventional wisdom, the marketing message, the well-traveled path of the snow sled. I had questioned The Ronald Reagan Story. You'd think that I'd gone and cut the nose off a koala bear and then pushed the tip of a burning cigar into the open wound.

Trugop432: @BeckIsALib If you think Reagan is a Moderate, sorry, but you're a political moron.

BeckIsALib: @Truegop432 I grew up with Reagan as Gov. of CA- He was a fiscal conservative/social mod through his 84 re-election. All else is myth.

And sometimes 140 characters just aren't enough:

BeckIsALib: @Truegop432 I would add that "moron" is just more name calling; if you're not interested in real conversation then just don't respond.

He came back with:

Trugop432: @BeckIsALib "Moron" is not always name-calling. I used it purposely, because you know damn well we were talking about Reagan as President.

I took a minute to look up the word "moron." Perhaps I'd been wrong all this time and the word had a kinder, gentler definition. Apparently not. Dictionary.com defines the epithet as "a person who is notably stupid or lacking in good judgment," while Merriam-Webster's says that a moron is "a person affected with mild retardation" and goes on to add an additional gloss, defining the word as "offensive." So, yes, @Truegop432, it *is* always name calling.

He wasn't done, though; he, too, needed more than 140 characters to make this particular point:

> Trugop432: @BeckIsALib I'll respond whenever the hell I feel like it--if you don't like it, block me, MORON.

Gee. Now I wasn't merely a "moron," but a "MORON." My get-the-last-word gene[112] kicked in; it took some willpower just to soften the response I eventually sent:

> BeckIsALib: @Truegop432 My point is that he stayed moderate into his 2nd term. He even appointed two moderates to the Supreme Court.

He came back with a classic cognitive dissonance dodge, casting luck, karma, fate, and whimsy as the bad guys rather than arguing evidence:

> Trugop432: @BeckIsALib The Court appointment is little better than a crap shoot; plenty of allegedly conservative justices turned out otherwise.

And then his classy finale:

> Trugop432: @BeckIsALib Don't know what your political persuasion is; I can't be bothered to look but you certainly act like LIB, trying to silence me.

---

[112] I have no proof that this propensity is genetic, but my grandfather had it, as did my father and three of my siblings. So—anecdotal or not—the evidence has me convinced.

Curious, I double-checked my tweets: nothing in there about trying to silence him, just a basic request for a *soupçon* of politeness. Is that where we've come to? Does "disagree" now mean "silence?"

I also fired off a short tweet intended to correct his mistaken belief that I'm a liberal. I doubt it made any difference. I never heard from him again.

I guess there's just no point in having conversations with people who refuse to let facts get in the way of the truth. He's swallowed the Reagan myth and the Republican manifesto built around it. @Trugop432 has now internalized that mythology, built atop his own prejudices, and has baked it into his own personal manifesto that he now broadcasts repeatedly in the 140-character marketplace of ideas.

WEEK ELEVEN:
SHAMES PEOPLE PLAY

G lenn Beck is going twenty-first century.

Forget Fox: that's old-fashioned media. Glenn's planning GBTV.com, an entirely fluid virtual world that will soon give him an even larger platform from which to warp the facts of history, tell us what to fear, beat up on the innocent, and separate us from a few bucks once in a while. I'll bet he's even working on an interactive version of his ubiquitous and omniscient blackboard. I'm sure the site will have direct links to Twitter, making it even easier for others to spread his messages for him. It'll be Glennbeck.com, Barry Bonds style, a steroidal outburst of conspiratorial and anarchistic lunacy.

Prior to the official launch, Beck is busy building buzz the way Lonesome Rhodes did, mixing gee-whiz homily with carefully crafted marketing messages aimed at driving curiosity and anticipation. In the meantime, though, he's stuck with old-fashioned radio and television, those same media used to perfect his *modus operandi*—outrageous behavior that he counts on others to amplify for him. The technique proves particularly effective when Beck turns abusive, something his long Top-40 history prepared him for very well. It's a tried and true routine: pick a public figure (it helps if the selectee already polarizes people), then pound away with a com-bination of cruelty and grossness just vile enough to ensure media interest. Add in the political factor and you've hit the trifecta at Aqueduct—which is pretty much what happened when he targeted McCain.

Not him. The other one.

Meghan McCain is the daughter of former GOP presidential nominee John McCain and his wife, Cindy Lou Hensley McCain.[113] Meghan blogs and writes, and not long ago released her first book, *Dirty Sexy Politics*, a memoir mixing stories of her father's campaign with her own opinions on social and political issues. She describes herself as a Republican who happens to have liberal social views.[114] "I am passionate about individual liberty," she writes in her book. "I believe in God and the church, but am as adamantly pro-life as I am passionate in my support of gay marriage." She deplores the loss of the GOP's center, wondering "how moderates like me would ever fit into their idea of what a Republican was, or should be." Not surprisingly, these are not attitudes that Beck and the other right-sided talking heads agree with.

Neither Glenn Beck nor the far right ever really supported John McCain except when he was the only alternative to the socialist, fascist, ultra-liberal, and foreign-born Barack Obama (and then only just barely). McCain, a Republican with moderate views, modeled the very definition of a RINO, a Republican In Name Only. He's been deemed a traitor more than once, as in this tweet:

---

[113] If you found yourself saying "Cindy Lou who?" then you've read too many Dr. Seuss books.

[114] Or, as we used to call it, a "Republican."

ChinaShopBull: @VenusShell What words would you like me to share about McCain? Sellout? Traitor? Neo-Marxist? Tell me when to quit.

The idea that someone—anyone—would characterize John McCain as a neo-Marxist is roughly equivalent to characterizing Shaquille O'Neal as "neo-short."

With John McCain still so reviled, all it takes is a public persona, a specific incident, and an accident of birth to get the Twitterverse all worked up about his daughter. Meghan is prey in the crosshairs, and Glenn Beck never misses a cheap shot taken at close range.

Recently Ms. McCain (along with a dozen or so other women, including actress and singer Brandy and former *Cosby* daughter Tempestt Bledsoe) appeared in a Public Service Announcement cautioning us about the risks of skin cancer. As many ads today do, the thirty-second spot drew attention largely through innuendo; all of the participants appeared to be nude while delivering their lines, which suggestively included sundry comments about the dangers of exposing oneself outdoors. The actual meaning of the less-than-subtle script was that these women would never consider heading out into the sun without a liberal layer of SPF-rich protection.

Meghan agreed to participate because the issue hits home for her; both her father and mother have fought melanoma, her father several times. From the sponsor's point of view, Meghan's stature—both as John's daughter and as editorialist and author in her own right—made her a logical choice for the PSA.

When the ad first aired, the Twitterverse—along with just about every other media outlet—went a bit nuts, which is likely what the sponsors both wanted and expected. The ad became a YouTube must-see and Meghan herself appeared both in print and on television talking it up. Given the content of the ad she certainly knew what kind of questions would be thrown her way, and she was obviously ready for them. Her controlled responses—built on a cute smile and a bit of eye-glimmer, typically ran as follows:

> McCainBlogette: Pundits in DC can calm themselves. I filmed a skin cancer PSA in a strapless juicy tube dress. All you can see is my collar bone.

She delivered the same message in similar flavors over several days, effectively garnering extra press both for the message and for herself. Pretty smart, actually. As a bonus, the ad, in going viral, provided a bit of lift for its sponsor, the new Style Network. That's a place I think Ms. McCain fits exceedingly well. Whatever else you may think about her, the girl's got style.

To Glenn Beck's delight, the girl's also a little zaftig.[115]

With his sights lasered on the cheap shot, Beck reacted on air with the kind of bile reminiscent of his early radio days. In a less-than-gracious bit he played the audio from the PSA and then pretended to vomit every time anyone mentioned the words "Meghan McCain" and "naked" in the same sentence. The sound effects were not just limited to a bit of gagging, either. Listeners didn't have to strain to hear the sounds of splashing liquids. How's that for class.[116]

---

[115] Yiddish word meaning "having a full-rounded figure; pleasingly plump." Also a Jewish-style deli in Brookline, Massachusetts, a suburb of Boston. Apparently their Banana Stuffed French Toast is legendary and their knishes are to die for.

[116] I like to think I'm a reasonably nice person. I also like to think that I'm empathetic to the pain and embarrassment of others. I get an emotional twinge whenever one of the characters on *Glee* has her heart broken. I always feel for the cheated on. I routinely cry at the end of *You've Got Mail, Pretty Woman,* and *Fried Green Tomatoes.* I can't help myself. When I first heard Beck's piece, I felt for Meghan McCain in that same visceral way. So as much as she pretends strength, I have to believe that Meghan was hurting a little on the inside.

A May 12, 2011 *Hollywood Gossip* piece laid out the details:

> Sen. John McCain's daughter, alongside other stars, appear [sic] in the spot in various forms of nudity. The point is that we're naked without sunscreen.
>
> Beck was unmoved, feigning the urge to hurl. He sarcastically said he was feeling ill from too much of a good thing or maybe he was trying "to imagine John McCain naked with long blonde hair."
>
> "When I look at that, I think to myself, I get the point, put some clothes on," griped Beck, who suggested she wear a burka to "be extra safe."

Meghan McCain hit back, deriding Beck as "pathetic and extremely desperate for publicity."

The Twitterverse lapped it up like a lion licking the blood from a fallen gazelle. As many defended Beck as decried his behavior, and the sides lined up along easily predictable lines. The left gave us these:

> Bookseller12: Meghan McCain Lashes Back At Glenn Beck For Fat-Shaming.
>
> Scottishlass9: Meghan McCain says her father could kick Glenn Beck's a**.

And the right quickly responded:

> Questionjohn: This morning's big question: why does anyone listen to anything Meghan McCain has to say about any subject?

Walkingman98: McCain's Slut Daughter Like Totally Goes on Jay Leno's Totally Awesome Show!

The only difference between the two sides seems to be a pair of carefully placed asterisks.

08 80

Despite the shamefulness (and shamelessness) of what happened to her, Meghan McCain is a self-chosen public figure. She knows that she's fair game for any tasteless, absurd outsized comment or accusation thrown her way. The same is true of many others (including Beck himself), and both sides are routinely merciless in their attacks on *them* while sycophantic in their support for *us*. But that doesn't explain the bullying that befell Trig McCain, Sarah Palin's infant son, at the hands of a very far left, uber-liberal blog, Wonkette.com.

Born with Down Syndrome to a loving mother, Trig became the innocent centerpiece of a left-vs.-right attack on his mother and, at the same time, a lesson in the power we have when we find ourselves face to face with *too far*.

Jack Stuef, a freelance blogger and frequent contributor to the generally snarky Wonkette.com, took a cheap shot at Trig when he, Stuef, made fun of a poem written by a group of Palin supporters in celebration of the boy's third birthday. "Oh little boy," the poem went, "what are you dreaming about?" Stuef then answered the question with astonishing cruelty: "What's he dreaming about? Nothing. He's retarded." If that weren't enough, the website included a color collage that included a picture of Trig wearing a tiara above the words "Reagan II" while a stripper on a pole danced seductively just to the right of his baby-faced cheek.

The Twitterverse went ape-shit. Accusations of hate speech lined up like ravens on a power line waiting for carrion. Stuef was called out for his bullying behavior. Wonkette.com saw an unprecedented uptick in traffic as one surfer after another checked whether there was actual truth behind what they were hearing. Simple tweets spread the word:

Jenny412A: Wonkette Makes Fun of Trig Palin, Calls Him "Retarded."

A new hash tag emerged, #TrigsCrew, intended for use by all the outraged wishing to voice their support for the boy and his mom, and their loathing for Wonkette.com and its acidic blogger.

NoSaintMyself: Libs apparently only like kids that have lib parents. All the rest can go to hell. Especially conservative ones. #TrigsCrew

LibsBite: #YouKnowWhatsAnnoying? People attacking other people's children just because they're "different." #TrigsCrew It's SICK!

With the rapidity and breadth that only social media provide, a pulse emerged and then grew quickly into a movement. The Twitter-swell erupted, driving that movement, planting roots at lightning speed then watching as the outrage blossomed. The right went after not only Stuef and Wonkette.com, but after the site's sponsors as well. Trig's Crew proved themselves a powerful voice, rapidly publicizing the names of key advertisers. Frequent retweets urged the sponsors to stand up for principle or face an enormous viral backlash. Within days Papa John's, Huggies, The Vanguard Group, Bob Evans Farms, and Coldwell Banker dropped their Wonkette.com ads; others soon followed. The site found itself under both virtual and financial assault.

Stuef was quickly put on probation and just as quickly posted an apology (though some opponents called it a "non-apology"): "I regret this post and using the word 'retarded' in a reference to Sarah Palin's child," he wrote. "It's not nice, and is not necessary, but I take responsibility for writing it. For those who came and are offended by this post: I'm sorry, of course. But I stand by my criticism of Sarah Palin using her child as a political prop."

I'd have to agree with the whole "non-apology" thing. It's kind of lame, Jack.

Wonkette.com, in their press release announcing the punishment, reminded its audience that Stuef was merely a freelancer and that any contributor—even a freelancer writing parody or satire—must remain vigilant that something written might possibly be mis-construed by "random people on the internet."

Wonkette's characterization of the reaction as "random people on the internet" reeks of naivety and self-importance. What we saw was a reaction by a collective conscience that uniformly decided there was a line out there and that Stuef and Wonkette.com had crossed it. If these were random people on the internet, then you might as well call the London Symphony Orchestra random musicians on a stage.

The Twitter-propelled outrage demonstrated a very rare attempt to hold someone accountable for publicly shameful and bullying behavior. It's a response we're not used to seeing; the many that came to Beck's defense for his putdowns of Meghan McCain rep-resent the mainstream response to this kind of bullying. It's cheap, it's easy and apparently we're okay with it. And if it comes with a bit of screaming, all the better. The response to Stuef's uncalled-for abuse of Trig Palin was the exception, not the rule. I can still find hundreds of tweets like these...

AnnCoulter: We'd save $2.5 trillion if Michelle Obama ate lighter lunches.

AlaskaSnark: So Mrs. Palin, you're almost 50 years old. Are you planning on faking any more pregnancies? Just asking.

TalkingDog: If anyone has received naked pictures of Nancy Pelosi or Harry Reid, please let Matt Drudge know.

...before I find even one apology. And nobody is holding anybody accountable. Hiding behind anonymity and outsized freedom-of-speech claims means that everyone gets a bullhorn along with Harry Potter's cloak of invisibility. It's a coward's combination.

Stuef and Beck represent the new shame game, bullies who pick on easy (and often innocent) targets in order to whip up constituencies. They are supported and reinforced by each other, by our media ("mainstream" or otherwise), by our politicians, and by the partisan mob that travels the Twitterverse, all of us snapping and clawing at each other like crabs fighting for territory, using our verbal weaponry with little thought or care for civility.

We shouldn't feign surprise; shameful behavior is rampant yet somehow defensible, and the pundits almost always close ranks with their own. Ann Coulter can hint that John Edwards is a "faggot" and trust that Sean Hannity will draft the rhetoric necessary to justify her comments. David Shuster can be counted on to defend Keith Olbermann whenever Keith appears to go off his meds and gets caught in one of his now famous over-rants. It's the way they roll and it's what their audiences want. Apparently, a little bullying makes for good publicity and even better ratings. There may be a line drawn for the Trig Palins of the world, but there's so much bullying on this side of the line that it barely matters that some attacks may be out of bounds.

I'm not sure when bullying emerged as the key currency in our political dialogue, but look around you anywhere: it's unavoidable.

Shameful behavior runs rampant, especially in the Twitterverse where it's both easy and anonymous. We exhibit it, we hunt it out in others, we broadcast it, we revel in it. It's not just about sharing good gossip anymore; we don't simply hang out at Starbuck's and swap suspicious little stories with good friends while sipping lattes and munching on overpriced biscotti. Instead we create, spread, and embellish whatever truth we care to invent, sometimes lacking even a basic kernel of decency, and then we cast it to the wind, knowing that whatever we've said will sooner or later fall upon eager ears. And we love it. There's a reason why more people watch *Entertainment Tonight* than CSPAN, why so many people know Lindsay Lohan's name but not John Boehner's.

We live in a time when our leaders, pundits, talking heads—even we ourselves—continually look for ways to pick on each other, embarrass each other, and score some cheap points before an ever-fickle audience, all without any accountability. With every listener a broadcaster and every broadcaster a pundit, any logorrheic comment amplifies logarithmically. All we can do is wait it out and try to find those few people buried in the crowds who are willing to talk about something else, or—on those very rare occasions—encourage the public forum to scream "Enough!"

ଔ ଓ

How's this for irony:

Senators Introduce Federal Anti-bullying Law
WASHINGTON, D.C. — U.S. Sens. Robert Casey, D-Pa., and Mark Kirk, R-Ill., announced their bipartisan introduction of a federal anti-bullying law Tuesday.

Talking with reporters via conference call, Casey said H.R. 2262, known as the Safe Schools Improvement Act, would help prevent what he considered the "ultimate betrayal of a child."

"This bill is a crucial step toward ensuring that no child is so afraid to go to school that he or she stays home for fear of bullying," said Casey. "I am pleased to introduce the Safe Schools Improvement Act to help ensure that every child receives a quality education that builds self-confidence."

That's right: in a time where television, radio, newspapers, and the internet are awash in such behavior, our leaders have decided that bullying is hurting our kids. They shouldn't have to endure it any longer. It has to stop.

Pot and kettle, anyone?

In addition to the federal statute introduced by Casey and Kirk, several states are now introducing legislation that would either create new anti-bullying laws or improve on laws already on the books. As of 2011, forty-six states have some form of no-bully laws, all graded on an A-to-F scale; eleven have an "A++" rating while three— Michigan, Hawaii, and Montana—linger with a grade of "F." Bully-police.org, an organization whose sole mission is to bully as many states as possible into passing anti-bullying legislation, keeps track of these things for us.[117]

New Hampshire (where I live) is one of those super-duper A++ states, having recently upgraded an anemic "C" law (originally passed in 2000) with HB 1523, "AN ACT revising the pupil safety and violence prevention act" whose "sole purpose is to protect all

---

[117] The nation's GPA, for those curious, is 2.9, or just below a "B." If you're interested in how these admittedly subjective grades are determined, you can see the list of criteria at their website, www.bullypolice.org.

children from bullying and cyber bullying, and no other legislative purpose is intended." The act-revising (and randomly capitalized) ACT goes on to define bullying as behavior that causes physical harm to a pupil or the pupil's property, causes emotional distress to the pupil, interferes with a pupil's educational opportunities, creates a hostile educational environment, or substantially disrupts the orderly operation of the school.

If you look at the current statistics on bullying, legislation like New Hampshire's appears warranted. Bullyingstatistic.org reports that, for the year 2009, roughly one-third of all teens experienced some kind of bullying. That's a big number. But when you dig a bit deeper into what those numbers mean, all of our lawmaking starts to look like an overreaction. The statistics show that 20 percent of those bullied were "made fun of," 18 percent had "rumors or gossip spread about them," 6 percent were "threatened," and 5 percent were "excluded from activities they wanted to participate in."

Or, as I like to call it, "childhood."

The report does point out that 11 percent of victims experience some sort of physical abuse, but that's mostly tripping, shoving, and spitting, not exactly the stuff of which police lineups are made. Once again we've proven ourselves a society prone to the knee-jerk, imagining zebras when we hear horses and designing our way into convoluted solutions that cause bitter dissent and disagreement along with all the new rules and policies, none of which seem to actually address the kids and their problems.

Anti-bullying efforts have even reached Facebook. Over 600 people have joined a group that calls itself F.A.B.L.E.—which stands for Federal Anti-Bullying Legislation, USA.[118] The group, founded by a New Jersey woman named Lin Clendenny, has the dual goals of awareness and petition, believing that "we need a federal anti-bullying

---

[118] The name apparently created by the acronymically challenged.

law in the United States." The group's icon is a squirrel wearing a battle helmet and holding a bazooka, overlaid with the classic "no" image—a circle with a diagonal line running through it—and bottomed by the tag line "Say No To Bullying."

A squirrel with a bazooka? Seriously?

The Facebook entries consist mostly of announcements, requests to sign petitions, and occasional testimonials from those who grew up under a bully's dark stare but have since overcome those fears. "October is antibullying [sic] month," one entry tells us. "October 4th is blue shirt day…Please wear blue on that day; we need to stop the bullying now!!"

I've joined the group so I can follow some of their discussions, but I can't say that I fully agree with their mission. While the site offers horrific tales (including stories of a twelve-year-old boy set afire while at a friend's house and another of a boy hit with a bleach-filled water balloon), I have a difficult time understanding how passing legislation is really going to make a difference. Children don't learn from the laws we lay down; they learn from role models: parents and teachers, religious and political leaders, celebrities and pundits. We are all of us them.

There is real danger out there for kids; it's not the water balloon prank but the bleach we need to worry about. Violence, bigotry, and hatred show up every day. Homophobia and racism continue to drive too many people, and such fears and emotions—when coupled with childhood's immaturity—can too often lead to tragedy. But that's not bullying. Desensitizing ourselves to serious incidents like these simply by labeling them with the juvenile-sounding "bullying" descriptor is a mistake. Perhaps it's simplistic to think that there's a difference between spitting and setting someone on fire, but to me the former is annoying while the latter is aggravated assault.

The growing number of smaller incidents, those simpler things that immerse all children at one time or another, come from something different, something we don't want to admit to ourselves: we're just not that nice anymore. If more and more of our kids increasingly exhibit such behavior, then perhaps it's time we admit that our kids merely reflect the society they're growing up in, the society that we've built for them.

You can't legislate niceness back into the culture. "Legislating" is not a synonym for "parenting" or "educating," nor should it be. The way forward is to demand civility of ourselves and those around us, to answer all bullying with the same reaction we did when Wonkette.com trashed Trig Palin. We don't need state and federal legislators to tell us how to handle bullying, and we certainly don't need cryptic and ambiguous definitions buried in something called HB 1523 for us to know—and for our parents and teachers to know—when lines have been crossed.

03 80

Twitter and other social networks make it easy not to be nice, offering both a coward's anonymity and a preacher's pulpit; as a result they take an unfair share of the criticism for contributing to our not-so-nice culture. But technology is mechanism, not cause, and there have been—and always will be—ways for the mean to be mean.

In the summer of 1972 I went steady[119] for a very brief time with an incredibly attractive girl named Livvy. She and I would meet at the Gardner Park pool a few days a week to swim, meet with friends, and occasionally sneak behind the hot dog stand for a few chaste kisses. It was a time of early exploration but not much more, and five or six weeks later it was over. No drama, no scene. We were just two kids who bounced off each other briefly then went our separate ways.

---

[119] For those too young to recognize the term, going "steady" was sort of the opposite of "friends with benefits." You were more than friends, but there were almost no benefits.

Then the shitstorm started.

Livvy's family, the Rosens, owned a local Baskin-Robbins franchise, one that I and my friends frequented and that my step-father patronized at least twice a week in order to replenish our freezer's ever-diminishing supply of Jamoca® Almond Fudge ice cream. I showed up to school one day and Gail, Livvy's sister, asked me to stop making those calls to the store.

"What?"

"Stop calling the store. It's not funny."

"What are you talking about?"

"I said it's not funny. Just stop, okay?"

I had no idea what she was talking about. Livvy wouldn't even look at me and when I stopped for ice cream on the way home a couple of days later, her parents refused to serve me and asked me to leave the store. Someone—and to this day I've no idea who—decided to make prank calls to the store using my name. They called repeatedly, two or three times a day, for weeks. Nothing I could say or do would convince them that it wasn't me, and I was never allowed in the store again. My stepfather asked me about it because the Rosens asked him about it. I think he sort of believed me only because I pleaded with him, and he knew I wasn't a good liar.

Several years later and now nearly a high school graduate, I still couldn't get Gail or Livvy to speak to me. Both still believed I had made those calls.

Such was the seventies equivalent of "cyber bullying." The only thing that's changed today is the scale, yet we've chosen to treat it as a new problem, one that is incredibly serious and requires the intervention of not just local authorities, but state and federal governments:

EBLivinLarge: Let's see if the House Judiciary Comm. can get to work on the first federal anti-bullying legislation. Updates to come.

MassMess: Sen. Scott Brown slammed for not appearing in anti-bullying video.

MinnLib: Michele Bachmann is anti-gay and doesn't like anti-bullying legislation, and her district has a high teen suicide rate. Hmm.

With social media an easy target for those mining causes, sites have predictably emerged that offer advice on cyber bullying, each with barely different riffs on the same theme. They largely provide trivial suggestions for parents and teachers, each one more facile than the last. Surfnetkids.com, a generally wonderful site with guidance, advice, and suggestions for parents on many important topics, is less effective on the subject of cyber bullying, offering only simple homilies like, "If you want cyber bullying to stop, you have to refuse to pass along cyber bullying messages," and "Don't talk or chat online with anyone besides your closest friends," and "Talk to your parents." They also admonish kids, reminding them that, "If you wouldn't say something in person, you should not say it online." Such guidance seems less like practical advice and more like the comic strip "Goofus and Gallant" from *Highlights*, the magazine left lying out in pediatric waiting rooms with half of the Hidden Pictures already circled in crayon and at least one page torn out.

The artless sermons that Surfnetkids.com and other, similar, sites provide are unlikely to make any real difference, divorced as they are from real day-to-day behaviors. I remember how school friendships constantly shifted: today's best friend was tomorrow's silent treatment. Does this kind of advice really help when an ex-friend decides to spread a rumor or when an embarrassing photo goes viral? Perhaps paying attention to the modeled behavior is what's needed. Surfnetkids.com would be more helpful if they gave advice like this:

"Hey, kids! If you want bullying to stop, next time you hear Daddy yelling at a telemarketer, ask him why he needs to be so mean!"

Undoubtedly Twitter, Facebook, and other social networks represent a sea change in the way societies (and the people within them) communicate—and that includes our kids. These raucously uncontrollable worlds, generated through culturally disruptive technologies, require new ways of thinking if we are to effectively incorporate them into our culture. New behaviors—and old behaviors performed in new ways—will take hold and spread, and for every one that does there will be millions of opinions, hundreds of organizations and, unfortunately, the occasional tragedy that screams at us to wake up, to change, to care in meaningful ways. The danger we face is in overreacting (or reacting with simplicity) to a complex problem.

I concede that cyberspace has changed the landscape, but the vast bulk of what has the nation up in arms is not fundamentally different than what we went through years ago. Race, gender, sexual orientation, and disabilities were all around back then, too. In some cases the slurs were worse. There's just more of it now, and I believe that the increase in incidents is a direct result of how we as adults now choose to behave. Our kids are simply modeling the behavior we continually prove acceptable.

Don't like what someone is saying? Just insult them. It's easier than engaging in any meaningful conversation:

SevenTwoSeven: Tea Baggers have Satan on speed dial...

Is there someone who doesn't agree with you? SHOUT AT THEM IN CAPITAL LETTERS AT THE TOP OF YOUR VOICE:

NotTakinIt: When ANYONE chooses to come to America and CHOOSES to become a citizen you adopt the Laws of OUR land, NOT YOUR CRAP!

Are the facts giving you trouble? Just replace them with your own version of the truth until you get others to believe it:

ArthurS421: John Kyl never misspeaks? "90% of Planned Parenthood's funding is for abortion" was "Not intended to be a factual statement."

As David Denby points out in *Snark*:

> "The internet will quickly turn snark into meme…The phrase, the insult has an existence in the media (someone said it, didn't he?), so it can be referred to, combined with other items, revived, denounced, dismissed as old news, and so on. The false item, made memorable by snark, passes through the entire cycle of media life. This is known as the 'national conversation.'"

It's what we do, and when I say "we" I mean America. Our responses are outsized, overlarge, and insistent. Among the Million Man Marches and the calls to Restore Honor and the Sarah Palin bus tours how can anyone just talk, just have a conversation? The shortest distance between two points is no longer a straight line; it's loudness. And we're shouting loudly enough for our kids to hear.

We talk about our laws and our kids as if they're separate from ourselves. They're not. As long as an elected representative can shout down the President of the United States with accusations of "You lie," as long as every Town Hall meeting becomes a designated showcase for screaming and media coverage, as long as every parent treats their own opinions as holy, and as long as we pay people like Glenn Beck tens of millions of dollars every year to act this way, then our children are behaving exactly as we've raised them to behave.

WEEK TWELVE:
TWEETS AND CHiRPs

Sometimes a metaphor slaps you in the face so hard that you simply have to pay attention.

I'm sitting on the couch next to my wife, having my first cup of coffee and watching *Good Morning America*. On one side of a split-screen Sam Champion delivers cheery weather-related banter from somewhere in Times Square, while behind him members of the crowd wave signs scribbled with forgettable sayings. There's something about the Great State of Ohio on one of them, but the rest of the message remains partially hidden behind a grandmotherly looking woman. Another placard extends an already overused trope by insisting that Geena, Maria and Alice love *Good Morning America*.

From her studio couch Robin Roberts smiles and says something cute, words she's likely said umpteen times before. Sam giggles and then kicks it back to Robin, who immediately shifts into her now-for-something-serious voice before passing the verbal baton to George Stephanopoulos, formerly the White House Communications Director under Bill Clinton and now Robin's co-anchor. George introduces his upcoming story, a live interview with former Pennsylvania Senator Rick Santorum.

Santorum, yet another extreme right member of the GOP parade with his sights set on the Oval Office, stands in front of the courthouse in Somerset, Pennsylvania. He's dressed in a blue blazer and a light blue open-collared shirt. The location is symbolic; it's where his grandfather immigrated to after fleeing a fascist Italy back in 1935. Santorum stands with a smile on his face while listening to the same thing we do: Stephanopoulos' brief and bland review of an ordinary political career. Behind the former senator, the courthouse steps are in the early stages of decoration, a *sanctum Santorum* in preparation for a formal press conference scheduled later that day. To no one's surprise Rick Santorum is officially getting into the race and, in keeping with the latest trend (and having previously announced to announce), he's now sort of announcing while not really announcing until his upcoming announcement.

Over Santorum's left shoulder we see an artistic grouping of American flags positioned in a flowerbed. Up the middle of the courthouse steps runs a railing; though currently unadorned, I can imagine the bunting that will wrap it by the time the press arrives. The most prominent display is a group of red, white, and blue balloons off to Santorum's right, running along the edge of the steps, scores of balloons, organized into stripes, bound together and framing the scene with a tapestry of patriotic color. At the top of the steps the balloon wall is tied to a pole standing in a weighted container.

The trite intro complete, Stephanopoulos starts the interview with a couple of softball questions that Santorum lofts easily into the seats, saying nothing anyone doesn't expect him to say. Yes, he's "in it to win." Yes, he sees "a path to the nomination" despite the trouncing he took in his last senatorial contest. And, yes, he's "very excited about this opportunity." Stephanopoulos gets slightly more aggressive when he reads a couple of questions from viewer emails, but Santorum stays with his talking points, all of which sound like the same pabulum any candidate feeds the electorate these days. He answers each question with aplomb, the smile never leaving his face. He even adds a little fist pump at one point, though it appears timid, like he's not quite sure the gesture is appropriate. I imagine Jessica, the Republican Club guest I met several weeks back, sitting at home with a genuinely wide smile, watching as her chosen candidate manifests her dreams.

I start to offer my opinions aloud, but when I look over at my wife, it's clear that she's struggling to maintain her patience. I'm pretty sure she wants to flip over to the The Weather Channel and would, too, if it weren't for my recently spiked interest in all things political and her unwavering support.[120] She takes another sip of coffee and invites Zoe, our mixed-breed rescue, over for some gentle ear scratching.

As we listen to the innocuous back-and-forth between Stephanopoulos and Santorum, a slight flutter at the side of the image draws my wife's attention. She stops the ear rubbing (much to Zoe's dismay) and taps me on the leg. One end of the balloon decoration has worked itself free and is starting to drift loosely in the breeze. The breeze becomes a gust and the balloons do more than flutter; they now begin to float away. My wife starts laughing and I quickly join her. We watch as a woman hustles up the steps, attempting to grab the runaway balloons much the way a teacher's aide might try to corral little Jimmy before he wanders off into the cloak room to eat a crayon. Now we're laughing even harder.

The interview continues.

The woman finally manages to herd the decoration, and for the next few minutes we can see only her white-strapped sandals peeking out from below the recalcitrant display, like those of some guilty lover hiding behind a curtain in a 1930's screwball comedy. All of

---

[120] Some might say "indulgence."

this happens with Santorum blissfully unaware that, off to his far right, carefully crafted plans are proving unruly.

For a few moments nothing more happens. Santorum and Stephanopoulos continue to chatter away, but my wife and I aren't even listening. Our eyes are riveted on that poor woman whose career aspirations undoubtedly never included miming a pole on national television. My laughter re-infects my wife and she starts laughing again, which only serves to get me going even harder. Slowly the mood wears off and we're just about back under control.

I'm all set to switch channels when a balloon pops.

My wife and I totally lose it. Two other people—another woman and a man judging by the shoes we can see rushing in from off screen—quickly imitate additional poles. Rick and George act like nothing's happened, but there's no way they didn't hear that balloon pop.

Santorum continues to babble and I continue to laugh, but now the laughter is mixed with a touch of disdain as Santorum rolls right along, talking now about the sanctity of life, Obama's socialist agenda, and the need for prayer. The smugness and surety leak from him like rusty water from an old faucet as he continues pretending that everything is just fine, thank you.

I'm uncomfortable in the same way that I was a couple of weeks ago when Jessica stood before that small group of fourteen Republicans and laid out Santorum's *bona fides*. He can say all the right words but underneath it what he's really saying are all the *far* right words. Santorum, like most of the GOP field today, looks to motivate through emotion rather than persuade through logic.

Santorum continues to pound away at his themes and his voice begins to rise slightly, both in volume and pitch. He's ruled by his own ideologies rather than by any rational view of governance and his disconnect from reality has never been so obvious to me as it is at this moment. He's an extremist who has decided somewhere along the way that winning means riling up more people than the next guy. There's no way we should ever allow such pretenders into leadership. I would so much prefer to hear from those with responsible and compassionate ideas, people who marry the best of fiscal intelligence with a growing social empathy. A bit conservative, a bit liberal—and a whole lot quieter. These people must be out there, and there must also be enough of a constituency to elect them. They need finding.

Another balloon pop, anyone?

 C3 ED

Glenn Beck remains rather quiet these days, though I can just barely hear the hissing from off to my right, a sound that reminds me of a steam pipe about to crack. Current Beckian news continues to center on his latest ventures in new media, Old Jerusalem, and his upcoming book, *The Original Argument: The Federalists' Case for the Constitution, Adapted for the 21st Century*. Sounds like a real page-turner.

The last few years have been very good to Glenn Beck. Despite his continued attempts to paint himself as a regular guy, he is anything but. According to a *Forbes* article from April 2010, Beck made roughly $32 million in the last year and *Business Insider* reports that his current annual income is upwards of $40 million. It brings to mind Orwell's famous line from *Animal Farm*: "All animals are equal, but some animals are more equal than others."

The income allows Beck and his family to live quite well, certainly better than I do. Until April 2011 Beck owned an impressive piece of property in a very wealthy community, Ponus Ridge, in New Canaan, Connecticut which, according to *CNN Money* is the single richest community in America. Dana Milbank, author of *Tears of a Clown: Glenn Beck and the Teabagging of America*, writes that Beck had a "sixteen-room neo-Colonial mansion on Ponus Ridge, which he purchased in 2005 for $4.25 million." The property has nearly three acres, borders a reservoir and is within easy reach of eighty-five different two-year and four-year colleges and universities, 403 golf courses, 2,500 restaurants, sixty-six libraries, nineteen museums, and more than one hundred bars. Plus, residents have lower than average rates for both body mass index (BMI) and diabetes. Sounds like a pretty nice neighborhood.

Beck also owns a place in New York City, probably just because he can. His next destination (now that the Connecticut property has finally sold after nearly eighteen months on the market) is as yet undisclosed, though rumors abound. It's been reported that he's moving to Texas, to the mountains of North Carolina, to Denver, and to the Syfy Channel.

Just to be clear: Glenn Beck says he's just one of us and routinely bashes liberal elites, suggesting that they lack a moral center and are out of touch with the way real people live. I always wondered why he (and others) didn't just say "elite," but now I know why the term requires a modifier—because there are plenty of conservative elites, too. They just don't want you to know it.[121]

Having all that money has given Beck plenty of time to consider his empiric strategy, all of which began with the premier of *The Glenn Beck Show* on the Fox News Channel back in 2009, one night before President-Elect Obama's inauguration. Beck's first guest was Sarah Palin, and Beck fought back a few tears as he told his audience how he and Governor Palin shared a common trial: both have a special-needs child. He then welcomed her with a few generous compliments.[122] Next topic? Obama, of course.

---

[121] Other conservative elites include Rush Limbaugh, with an estimated annual income well in excess of $50 million, and Sean Hannity, another "regular guy," who earns north of $20 million. How far north is hard to say.

[122] Actually, he referred to her as "one hot grandma."

By March of that same year even the generally liberal *Los Angeles Times* grudgingly acknowledged that Beck's show was a hit. In an article entitled "Fox News' Glenn Beck Strikes Ratings Gold by Challenging Barack Obama," *The Times* reported that Beck's audience had already topped two million viewers. "That made Glenn Beck the third most-watched program in all of cable news for the month, after Bill O'Reilly's and Sean Hannity's evening shows," the article said. Beck wasn't surprised though. "People know in their gut that something's not right," he's quoted as saying. "They're not getting the truth."[123]

Beck soon realized that constant exposure through television, radio, and print simply wasn't enough for him, and so on top of all that Beck devoted the next two-plus years to a series of projects (his Restoring Courage rant in Jerusalem only the latest) aimed at sharing his messages with an ever more vocal community of ardent worshipers. For Beck, people "getting the truth" is best accomplished on a grand scale.

His most famous project, the "Restoring Honor" rally held on the Mall in Washington, D.C. in August of 2010, drew a largely right-wing crowd estimated at anywhere from 78,000 to 500,000 (depending on whether you choose to believe the science or the spin).[124] The crowd listened to Beck and a slate of guests (including the

---

[123] [Sigh]

[124] Crowd estimates are generally done through a combination of aerial and ground photography combined with tested mathematical algorithms. The only scientific analysis of crowd size for this particular event came from AirPhotosLive.com, which estimated the crowd at 87,000, +/- 9,000, a believable number unless you're one of those people who is absolutely positive that this is just another conspiracy by the lamestream liberal media, in which case who am I to bother you with something as irrelevant as mere data. Side note: crowd estimates used to be done through public sector sources, but this is increasingly rare ever since Louis Farrakhan threatened to sue the United States' Park Police for estimating the size of his "Million Man March" at roughly 400,000.

omnipresent Sarah Palin) lecture lovingly about God, America, Lincoln, Moses, and George Washington, all while participating in a schizophrenic salute to the military, Christianity, and St. Louis Cardinals first baseman Albert Pujols.[125]

Prior to honor's restoration, Beck's most fervent and awe-inspiring effort was the one he termed "The 9/12 Project." Begun in March 2009 with the goal of bringing us back to where our national spirit was the day after the 9/11 attacks, Beck urged his followers to recall a time when "we were not obsessed with red states, blue states, or political parties. We were united as Americans, standing together to protect the values and principles of the greatest nation ever created." "9/12" also stands for the Nine Principles and Twelve Values that serve as dual cornerstones for the project. Several of these arrive coated in irony, coming as they do from Beck. Principle Three, for example, states that "I must always try to be a more honest person than I was yesterday," and Value Eleven describes "Personal Responsibility."[126]

The 9/12 Project continues to thrive, an Astroturf campaign that somehow blossomed and grew anyway. The Project's website lists dozens and dozens of meet-ups across the country with representation in all fifty states and the District of Columbia. It boasts of educational programs and reading rooms, and is in every way a professional and thoroughly modern organization. They even sell t-shirts. There is that one problem with facts, though, and I advise

---

[125] Beck gave out "civilian" medals of honor, and Pujols won the "Hope" award for the Pujols Family Foundation, the vision of which is to "promote awareness, provide hope, and meet tangible needs for families and children who live with Down syndrome." Pujols, subsequently forced to defend his appearance, saw the event as a chance to describe the role God plays in his life and to bring the message of his foundation before thousands.

[126] There's no real reason for this footnote other than to give you time to finish laughing.

anyone interested to proceed with caution. While the Principles and Values are, on the surface, laudable, there lies beneath them an encouragement toward the same ultra-conservative ideals and behaviors that litter the ground everywhere Beck goes. Message forums routinely echo the misconceptions and lies one hears on talk radio every day, and 9/12 rallies are often haunted by signs linking Obama with everything from socialism to Hitler.

Now Beck is taking his $40 million show to Israel and the internet.

Glenn Beck continues to find ways to both entertain us and to impact the political conversation. He must be tremendously influential; after all, he tells us so. Very few on the right will challenge him so they, too, must think Beck important. The guy even managed to get himself a cover story in *The New York Times Magazine*.

Sorry: I'm just not buying it anymore.

Yes, it's true that Beck can launch books up the bestseller lists, and yes, it's true that he can bring new (and often harmful attention) to people like Van Jones[127] and Frances Fox Piven[128]. It's also true

---

[127] Van Jones, the former Special Adviser for Green Jobs to the White House Council on Environmental Quality, is often the poster child for Beck's influence. Beck featured him on numerous programs, painting him as a Communist (which he previously had been), a Marxist (who really knows what that means anymore?), and a founder of the socialist group called STORM, "Standing Together to Organize a Revolutionary Movement (which is true, but Jones left the group long before joining the White House). Beck and others banged the guilt-by-association drum for quite a while until Jones finally felt forced to resign. I know I'm in the minority, but I'm not willing to give Beck all that much credit for what appears to have been a totally avoidable situation. The White House did a crappy job of vetting Jones and, whether qualified or not, anyone stupid enough not to anticipate the far right attacks should have been out the door with him.

[128] Frances Fox Piven, Professor of Sociology at the Graduate Center, City University of New York, became a favorite Beck target largely because of work she did with Richard Cloward, her husband and collaborator up until his death in 2001. The two developed a strategy for ending poverty based on collapsing modern welfare by enrolling as many people as possible into the system until it collapsed,

that a cottage industry has grown around him; hell, this book is part of it. But still, were his followers ever going to vote any differently than they do now? Apart from the rare conversion of someone like Victor Mooney (aka @ReaganStyle), how many minds has Beck really changed? And, if he hasn't changed any minds, then what's the big deal? We're back to my original description: Glenn Beck is just Uriah Heep with a clown's nose; he isn't that relevant to me anymore.

CB   BO

King Hiero II had a problem. Having recently given over quite a princely sum of gold to an artisan and instructing said artisan to craft a beautiful crown, the king was now second-guessing his own decision. Hiero wasn't the most trusting soul in the world (plus he'd heard a couple of rumors here and there) and was now worried that the artisan might perhaps have skimmed a bit, replacing some of the very valuable gold for some much less valuable silver. Hiero wanted to be sure, though, before he had the guy killed. Just to be fair and all.

---

thus forcing the emergence of a new model. The ideas, published as an article in 1966, came to Beck's attention back in 2009 and he latched onto the "collapse" part of the strategy and declared, in his show of August 24, 2009 that "once that system has collapsed, a new one is put in its place. Well, what system could possibly be ready to go? I don't know, but what better time — is there a better time to implement the 1960s radical ideology from scratch than when a president who has clearly said over and over again he's not a Marxist, couples himself with a far left-leaning Congress and advisers who are self-proclaimed Marxists, socialists, and communists?" Beck took one article from a fifty-plus year career and decided to list Piven as "one of the nine most dangerous people in the world." He used her words out of context to demonize an intelligent and respected sociologist. Beck has kept at Piven on and off for nearly two years now; Piven has received death threats and may have been the victim of several attempts on her life. Beck hasn't backed off, or even urged his listeners away from violence specifically aimed at Piven. Unlike Van Jones, no one could have seen this one coming, and Beck's behavior is clearly inciteful. Still, as much as I realize that Beck has had an enormous impact on her personally, the situation doesn't argue for Beck's broader influence across the political landscape.

Given that all of this took place more than 2,200 years ago and that most mathematics hadn't yet been invented, the king wasn't sure how to check out his suspicions. He had neither instrument nor method for determining whether the craftsman was really an honest man or had decided instead to fund his retirement out of Hiero's largesse.

Enter Archimedes. Born circa 287 BC in Syracuse, a Sicilian seaport city, Archimedes was a mathematician, inventor, physicist, and astronomer. His life was either very boring or very exciting, the verdict depending entirely on your own opinion of how fascinating it must have been to calculate the value of pi. He also invented a heat ray which he claimed could be used to focus the sun's force on approaching ships and thereby cause them to burst into flames. This makes Archimedes rather like the Martians in H.G. Wells' *The War of the Worlds,* only not as ugly.

Given that Archimedes had all these mathematical skills, Hiero decided that he, Archimedes, would be the perfect guy to solve his, the king's, problem. Knowing how testy (and persuasive) the king could be, Archimedes accepted the challenge. He struggled for a bit, unsure of how to approach the issue, then one day while in the bath, it hit him: equal volumes displace equal amounts of water. Since silver is lighter than gold, an equal weight would yield a higher volume and, therefore, should displace a greater amount of water.

As the story goes, Archimedes leapt out of the bath and ran through the streets naked, screaming "eureka" over and over, having suddenly solved one of the greatest mathematical mysteries of the age.

Great story. Only it never happened.

Archimedes wrote down pretty much everything, probably because he knew he was a smart guy and wanted to make sure others knew it, too. Many of his works—with scintillating titles like "On the Measurement of a Circle," and "The Quadrature of the

Parabola"—survive to this day and remain unread by pretty much everybody. But those few who do admit to reading Archie's works tell us that the "eureka" story never shows up.

Given the fascinating nature of the discovery, I would have thought that it would have at least been scribbled down in a margin somewhere. Why isn't it there? It's because there was no cry of "eureka," no Archimedean moment. That's not the way the world works, not even in ancient times.

Epiphany. Discovery. Revelation. Inspiration. It doesn't matter what you call it, it's not real except in retrospect, as a good story, as mythology. Moments of understanding develop and evolve. Self-definition arrives slowly. That's what happened with me. As I've listened, watched, conversed, and tweeted about politics over the last couple of months, as I've followed Glenn Beck from one outrage to another, I've come to realize there's a gap to be filled between the vocal extremes, between today's liberal and conservative descriptions and the reality of what I believe I—and many others—actually care about. Rick Santorum and his recalcitrant balloons merely surfaced my awareness.

I've been floating in this breach for a while now and it finally has a name. I rewrite my Twitter bio:

@BeckIsALib: Active Consiberal, a Republican who believes in fiscal responsibility and compassionate social policy, like the GOP did for 150 years.

I don't know what's going to happen now. I do know that this isn't about Glenn Beck anymore—if it ever really was. He's nothing to me, just an extra in a Molière comedy. In the long run he's not really doing anything to anyone, has no real impact. He's planted memes, certainly, but only in soiled soil. At this point in his career he may even believe everything he says—certainly he's spent enough years riding that snow sled through those same neural slaloms—but I'm still of the opinion that he's mostly a showman. But what Glenn Beck believes or doesn't believe isn't important. He convinces very few and wastes our time. He garners a lot of attention, but it's merely the same kind of attention we might give to Mr. Rogers or Pee Wee Herman, the giddy-eyed admiration of a mesmerized child. He's very loud and very visible, but so are many others.

What matters isn't the noise but the quiet; that's where the real sounds lay.

ೞ ೞ

BeckIsALib: I've changed my bio; I realize that my definition of conservative doesn't match the far right 25% of the GOP most common on Twitter.

ೞ ೞ

Too many people claiming today's Republican mantle aren't even real Republicans at all; they're far-right conservatives who have no patience for the rest of us, whom they consider RINOs— Republicans In Name Only.

It's why we need to claim our own mantle.

ೞ ೞ

BeckIsALib: I don't like being called a RINO; it's rude. Instead, I'm calling myself a #CONSIBERAL: a fiscal conservative and social moderate: a true Republican. Any others?

PoliteTParty: No 'moderate' Republican will get my vote in the primary.

BeckIsALib: @PoliteTParty Then you're dooming us to four more years of Obama; only a #consiberal voice can win.

PoliteTParty: @BeckIsALib RE: Your 'consiberal': just like McCain was, huh?

BeckIsALib: @PoliteTParty Yes. And that's a bad thing? McCain is a classic Republican, representing 150 years of party history. Not like today's CHiRPs.

jjj

There has always been room in both parties for those who are either more or less liberal, more or less conservative. Our two-party system virtually demands the welcoming preacher. Even the ultra-right and the extreme-left—those most often called "wingnuts" and "moonbats" in the Twitterverse—usually end up sharing the tent with those in their corresponding political party.[129] But today the traditional Republican Party is under siege and it seems that the only reason the extreme right doesn't break off and create a viable third party is because it's easier to redefine mine.

And it's starting to really piss me off.

Being a Republican, for example, isn't about gun control or abortion. It isn't about God and Christianity, or immigration or

---

[129] This despite the fact that there are actually many more than two parties in America. We have the Constitution Party, the Green Party, and the Libertarian Party. We have the American Third Position Party, the Modern Whig Party, and the Objectivist Party. But all of these (and more) have about as much influence on politics as the *Police Academy* movies have on modern cinema.

Hollywood. None of these are long-held Republican issues, issues of political philosophy. Abortion, for example, doesn't even appear in the GOP platform of 1968 despite the dramatic changes in abortion law in the mid- to late-sixties. It's not until 1972 that the party platform contains a plank on the subject, and the language used, while leaning pro-life, actually acknowledges and encourages debate on the subject. The so-called political issues of today's Republicans are more accurately the conservative issues of the far right. Nor is Republicanism about who can throw down the most gauntlets, force the first blink, or rewrite history to suit today's agenda. Those are techniques of the extremists, and they succeed only in putting our government, our economy, and our way of life at risk.

I call these people, these Republican masqueraders, *CHiRPs*— Conservatives Hijacking the Republican Party. And I dearly wish they'd stop.

ଓ ଞ

JimintheMiddle: Where are the moderate Republicans, Republicans with some sense? This far right mess has made me turn a deaf ear to anything GOP.

BeckIsALib: @JimintheMiddle Moderate Republicans are here! I'm trying to find them, too. We are the #consiberal voice, and are actually most of the party!

JimintheMiddle: @BeckIsALib I would love to meet them... then maybe we could actually do some productive things in society!

ଓ ଞ

Question: Who was the last Consiberal president, one who exemplifies the classic Republican principles of fiscal conservatism and social moderation?

Answer: William Jefferson Clinton.

ଓ ଯ୦

BeckIsALib: @RWwatchMA @ScottBrownMA I think moderate Republicans should rage. CHiRPs are taking over the party, and we need a #consiberal voice.

BeckIsALib: Anyone who agrees with the #consiberal message, please RT. We're for fiscal conservatism and social moderation.

ଓ ଯ୦

BeckIsALib: @Jeffright34 If the GOP puts up a far right candidate there's no chance of victory; the far right represents only 25% of the GOP. We need a #consiberal or it's more Obama.

Jeffright34: @BeckIsALib The tea party types are more than 25%. The traditional GOP might have lost half their base. Not many say "I am a Republican" anymore.

Jeffright34: If GOP puts up an establishment moderate candidate, I will vote 3rd party; so will millions of others. Could be the last election for the GOP as a political party.

ଓ ଯ୦

BeckIsALib: #CHiRP: A Conservative Hijacking the Republican Party. Won't even entertain conversation in the middle, hates anything left of Palin.

Symphony78: The Dems are counting on the Tea Party splitting support in the primaries and the GOP nominee being a new McCain, a melba toast establishment yawner.

BeckIsALib: @Symphony78 What you call "melba toast" I would call a #consiberal: fiscal conservative/social moderate (which is most of the GOP). That's what it'll take to beat Obama.

Symphony78: @BeckIsALib Hate to disagree with ya, bro, but that is what keeps losing.

BeckIsALib: @ Symphony78 '08 was an aberration; after Bush any Democrat would have won. If we nominate an ultra-con, you'll see Obama Republicans like '80 saw Reagan Democrats.

BeckIsALib: @Symphony78 I'd also argue that the Tea Party should be a separate party; I'd prefer to have my party back.

Symphony78: @BeckIsALib Your new word and theory is fun, but winning is actually simple. It takes plain spoken, unambiguous courageous leadership.

BeckIsALib: @Symphony78 We completely agree on that one. I'm actually hoping that Huntsman is the one; he's the closest to my #consiberal thinking.

ⓒⓢ ⓑⓄ

BeckIsALib: Palin, Bachmann, Santorum et.al. are CHiRPs: Conservatives Hijacking the Republican Party. The true GOP is #consiberal and we want our party back.

GOPSocialMedia: The only thing wrong with being a moderate in the Republican Party is that the Republicans hate you and so do the Democrats.

BeckIsALib: @GOPSocialMedia Too true. I believe, though, that there are many, many more of us #consiberals than people think.

ൠ ൠ

BeckIsALib: Latest poll numbers show #CHiRPs Palin and Bachmann getting slaughtered by Obama. Only a #consiberal has a shot right now.

ൠ ൠ

BeckIsALib: #Consiberal—a post-modern political creature.

ൠ ൠ

Googling the word "consiberal" returns 1,150 hits. Many of these are redundancies however; the actual count is considerably lower. I did find an accidental Facebook community page with six followers[130] and an article from the Cedar Park Church of Christ

---

[130] When you fill out your profile on Facebook, the system creates a community page for any term entered. A couple of people must have come up with the term "consiberal" and entered it into the "Political Views" field on their profile (as I have done.) The page has no posts, nor any indication as to who might have used the term.

entitled "Consiberalism," written back in 1973. However, in a world where the combined search term "conservative-plus-politics" returns thirty-five *million* search results, I doubt anyone would call the term "consiberal" widespread.

 times

BeckIsALib: A #consiberal accepts and respects that NOTHING is black and white; opinions are part of every argument.

BeckIsALib: A #consiberal believes in God and country, but doesn't get self-righteous about it. Disagreement doesn't mean wrong and right.

BeckIsALib: A #consiberal is someone who acknowledges that "beliefs" and "facts" are not the same thing, and always assumes three sides to any debate.

As Week Twelve comes to an end, I search Twitter for the word "consiberal" in the hopes that someone, somewhere has amplified the term. The results are remarkably consistent: every entry is mine. All this work, all this time, and I'm just now starting over.

Michael Charney

WEEK THIRTEEN:
BECK AND CALL

I'm tired, frustrated, and cranky, as brain dead as Newt Gingrich on a good day. It's June 10, just five days short of the Ides, and I can't say that I have much to show for all my efforts.

When I started twelve weeks ago, I saw the task ahead of me much as Sisyphus must have seen that damned boulder, as endless repetition colored by a self-deception wanting to believe that maybe today (or, at worst, tomorrow) success will arrive. Day after day I planted seeds in the Twittersphere only to see the vast majority die for lack of watering. A fistful of people warmed to the notion that Glenn Beck is more actor than not, but the greatest percentage of tweeps still think of Beck as they always have. They love him or hate him, hang on his every word or ignore him, marvel at his insight or laugh aloud at each uttered inanity.

Now, with Beck behind me, I feel less like Sisyphus and more like K., the protagonist from Franz Kafka's novel *The Castle*. K., summoned by mistake to serve as the land surveyor for a small village, wants only to find his way into the mysterious bureaucracy within the Castle in order to rectify the error. Yet despite all reasonable efforts he simply cannot penetrate the densely packed and imperfectly perfect system of rule. The mistake that brought K. to the village is clearly a mistake but cannot be a mistake because those in the Castle do not make mistakes. All attempts to undo what hasn't officially occurred end up thwarted by convoluted processes, errant communications, and outright falsehoods for which no one responsible is ever identified and no one accountable is ever held to task.

Fittingly, the novel remained unfinished when Kafka died.

CȜ ȢↃ

We're watching *Jeopardy*, a nice little metaphor for what's to come.

In a few moments I'll switch over to CNN. For the first time in my life I plan to watch a political debate from beginning to end; the event, the first of the New Hampshire primary season, may be the hottest ticket in town—which probably tells you as much about how many political junkies we have up here as how little there is to do.[131]

Final Jeopardy comes and goes, Alex Trebek lumbers through his goodbyes and handshakes, and I switch the channel. There are still two minutes of commercials to wade through so I get up to slice a pear and sprinkle some cinnamon on it, returning just in time to see the colorful high-definition debate graphics swoop across the screen. We settle in.

As the debate opens, seven candidates walk up to their respective podiums, each with a large smile and a small wave, appearing both casual and condescending in equal parts. From right to further right they are: Herman Cain, Tim Pawlenty, Ron Paul, Mitt Romney, Newt Gingrich, Michele Bachmann, and Rick Santorum. Six of the seven

---

[131] Before any other New Hampshire residents bring out the "if you don't like it here, then move" broom, let me say that I do like it here. But that doesn't mean it's a terribly exciting place. Lots of trees and stuff, sure. But the Mall of New Hampshire doesn't even have a bookstore.

have officially declared for the Presidency, all except for Michele Bachmann. Ten seconds later, though, she's no longer the exception, having chosen this moment and this venue to officially declare her candidacy. Now all seven are in the race. The only other major contender not present is Governor/Ambassador Huntsman, though he plans on announcing shortly and we Granite Staters will certainly see plenty of him in the upcoming months.

CNN's John King drew moderator duty for the event. He fires an opening salvo before getting started, warning all seven that he plans to firmly enforce the rules, particularly regarding time. He also reminds them that their answers shouldn't wander far afield from the questions asked. Good luck with that, John.

I feel for the guy, at least a little. He has a job no one envies: moderating political reporters, audience members, remote onlookers, and a Twitter feed, all while attempting to keep seven large egos in roughly equal balance. On top of that he's forced to ask a bunch of stupid questions designed to let us "get to know a bit more about the candidates," like when he asks Herman Cain, "Deep dish or thin crust?"

Despite King's best efforts, the Twitterverse wasn't terribly kind, as the post-debate timelines showed:

GOPHumor: OMG! THANK you, John King, for that hard hitting "Coke or Pepsi" question! Finally we have answers!!

Famousbro: How many words can King put into how many people's mouths?

Kingmaker: John King is a doucherocket.

Personally, I think he did okay, sort of like Wink Martindale bravely pretending that *Tic-Tac-Dough* is an exciting and challenging game show. Mr. King had to deal with much tougher contestants, though. The very nature of presidential candidacy demands an outsized personality, an instinct for pedantry, a desire for the spotlight, and incredibly white teeth.

Seven candidates dividing up roughly ninety minutes of actual debate time meant that they were each supposed to get about thirteen minutes, but that's only if they had elected to play fair. I didn't take a stopwatch to it, but I'm guessing Rick Santorum stole a bit of time from Newt, Pawlenty stole some time from Herman Cain, and Mitt stole some time from just about everybody.

Timing indiscretions, though, are just about the only indiscretions. The show was a regular love-fest, almost as if they'd all gotten together in the green room beforehand and agreed that nobody would run with scissors—unless they were pointed at President Obama. And that's what happened. Despite one or two attempts from Mr. King to liven things up, particularly with his reference to Pawlenty's portmanteau "Obamneycare," all the candidates followed the same playbook: economy horrible, jobs gone, Obama evil, Republicans magic. I was hoping for a bit of snark, frankly. These things get pretty boring when people remain polite.[132]

When I first sat down to watch, I took a quick personal inventory of my expectations, prejudices, preconceived notions, and biases. The candidates all came with baggage, but I had to acknowledge that most of it was mine, packed with internet conversations, sound bites, and clips from *The Daily Show*, and then handed over to them for carrying. Bachmann and Newt, in particular, were already caricatures in my mind, so it was important that I acknowledge and set aside those impressions if I were to give myself a fair shot at understanding these

---

[132] Said lack of excitement took its toll. My wife bailed less than halfway in, choosing instead to go upstairs and watch something on HGTV, probably having to do with a dangerously moldy bathroom.

people. I promised myself that I would try my damnedest to remain objective. I also decided that I wasn't going to think about who was "winning" the debate, having come to the conclusion long ago that it's a stupid question. Debates shouldn't be for winning or losing but for learning. I wanted to understand the candidates (at least as much as they would let me). I wanted to explore the way they thought, their sense of logic, and how they felt about issues important to them and to us. I know that's hard; they're trained to speak to polls and pundits and not to people, yet I felt that if I remained objective, observed closely and—most importantly—set aside my biases, then I might actually get there. I watched, listened, and took notes with as open a mind as I could muster and slowly the candidates became other that what I had prepared for.

I expected Michele Bachmann to say something stupid. She didn't. The Representative from Minnesota's 6th District proved herself intelligent, articulate, and passionate. While she rarely veered off script, she answered questions honestly, did not pander, and did not beg off from tackling hard questions on socially conservative issues, issues her handlers must have told her would likely not play well before the largely centrist New Hampshire constituency. In performing well she likely put to rest some of the criticisms that she's less a serious candidate than an aging extra from a George Romero movie, come again to eat the brains of any who veer too close. Still, she'll need to break out of her far-right corner if she plans to run any closer than a "nice try" second place.

Newt Gingrich also impressed me. Though I'd been aware of his strengths as an orator for some time, I was surprised by his sense of conviction. Evincing the aura of an elder statesman for most of the debate—someone who had been through the Clinton wars and emerged the better for it—he came across as the most collected and experienced of the bunch.

Then he blew it with the inevitable stupid Nazi analogy.

Weeks before, Herman Cain had gotten himself into a spot of trouble when he suggested that he wouldn't allow Muslims into a President Cain administration. The issue not surprisingly came up during the debate. Newt, never one to pass up an opportunity to insert himself into controversy, came up with this jingoistic yet scarily popular tirade:

> I am in favor of saying to people: If you're not prepared to be loyal to the United States, you will not serve in my administration. We did this in dealing with the Nazis and we did this when dealing with the Communists and both times it was controversial. And both times we discovered that, after a while, you know, there are some genuinely bad people who would like to infiltrate our country and we have got to have the guts to stand up and say "no."

For a moment I thought Newt had come under the spell of the long-dead Father Coughlin, the anti-Semitic priest whose FDR-era radio shows focused constantly on the need to root out Godless Communism from within the administration. Coughlin drew as many as 30-million into his paranoid net with each broadcast.

When the audience applauded, I realized that it wasn't only Newt possessed; Father Coughlin had taken over the entire room.

Herman Cain pretty much sidestepped the anti-Muslim question. In fact, he just about sidestepped every question. Clearly trying to widen his fan base with this, his New England coming-out party, Cain did himself no favors by harping on one single point over and over and over again until he started to sound like one of the adults in a Peanuts cartoon: wahh wahh *wahh*, wahh wahh *wahh*, wahh wahh.

"We need to work on the right problem."

"Let's look at solving the real problem."

"I'm a problem solver."

"The problem hasn't been solved."

"It starts with making sure we understand the problem."

It didn't matter what subject anyone talked about. It could have been immigration, health care, jobs, the value of the dollar, or the pattern of the White House china. In Herman's world we first argue about the problem before we even think of trying to solve it. If he used any of his microphone time to offer actual solutions then I must have missed it, distracted as I was by needing to scribble down all of his pithy problem quotes.

Cain disappointed me more than any other candidate, proving himself so deeply out of his league that I wonder at the sanity of those who advised him to get in the race. And while I respect the value that business experience brings to the presidency, being president is not like being the country's CEO. The buck may have stopped in the Oval Office back in Truman's time, but today the buck is all over the place; accountability and responsibility are as difficult to locate as a parking spot in Manhattan on Black Friday. A president without political experience—solid political experience—sounds like a set-up without a punch line and not something we should ever really consider.

The next morning, despite my personal admonition not to think in terms of winners and losers, I found myself tweeting about Cain:

BeckIsALib: #NHDebate: Worst performance: Cain, because the problem isn't the problem definition of the right problem or the problem's problem...

The other standout for me was Representative Ron Paul but again, not in a good way. He banged his "kill the Fed" drum a few times, as expected, then demonstrated his abysmal sense of geography when he said that we should "worry about our own borders rather than the border between Iraq and Afghanistan."[133] And Ron— can you please buy a suit that fits? And while you're at it, I've noticed that whenever you get excited you sound like Walter Brennan in *The Real McCoys* excoriating Luke for going too easy on the young-uns.[134] You might want to play back the tapes and—dag nab it— check it out for yourself.

My memory of the other candidates grew quickly fuzzy. I believe it was Tim Pawltorum or Rick Sanlenty or Tim Ricplenty who kept quoting its accomplishments as governor and/or senator and/or fiscal conservative and/or social conservative. The only thing I'm sure about is that it was male. And Mitt, the ostensible frontrunner, had only a single memorable moment: his announcement that the Boston Bruins were kicking the crap out of the Vancouver Canucks in the sixth game of the Stanley Cup Finals (though he used much less colorful language).

What I didn't hear from any of the candidates were words of moderation or compromise, something—anything—that might speak to the not-so-extreme segment of the GOP, the one so stunningly, disappointingly mute.

---

[133] I'm guessing he doesn't care much for the Department of Education, either.

[134] I'm seriously dating myself here. *The Real McCoys*, a sitcom starring Richard Crenna, Walter Brennan, and Kathleen Nolan, aired from 1957 to 1963. You can find clips on YouTube if you're curious. IMDB indicates that the show had exactly zero memorable quotes, though I particularly like "Mr. McCoy? Will you please get your nose out of my pie?" For trivia buffs, yes, this is the same Richard Crenna that later shows up in the Rambo movies and, with darkened brow, utters the line, "God didn't make Rambo. I made him."

ය ෨

Years ago we often heard and read about something called a "silent majority," a swelling electorate composed of quiet, thoughtful people who represented the true America, an America very different from the one described by those who stand before today's microphones and commandeer the national speech. The term has fallen into disuse but perhaps should be revived, echoing as it does a simpler and more even-tempered time.

Who are these people? A member of the silent majority is just an average person working hard to get through the day, worrying mostly about kids and jobs and mortgages. He listens to the news on the way to work, or maybe some retro rock from the eighties or nineties. She rides a crowded train into the city, one hand holding the back of a seat and the other holding a folded newspaper that she half-reads while thinking about her tweenage daughter and the upcoming and inevitable rebellion. He wakes before dawn to tend the farm animals and the fields while hoping for a ground-drenching rain that's long overdue. These are not people who care all that much about Sarah Palin's emails, Anthony Weiner's tweets, or Newt Gingrich's infidelities. They care about the price of food, the health of their parents, and the cost of a decent education. They care about culture and values and raising responsible kids. It's not that they're disengaged from the political landscape but rather that they're engaged in life: struggles and pleasures, likes and dislikes, days and nights. Many represent the consiberal voice, the vast majority of Americans who say and do little while the loudest eddies swirl.

Extremists make the airwaves tingle; Father Coughlin knew this, as do all of his progeny, from Glenn Beck to Ed Schultz. It's much more interesting to listen to rants than rationality and, judging from book sales and radio talk show lineups, there's more money in it, too.[135] Watching the news, surfing through blogs, and tweeting across the virtual world might make anyone think that the dominant profile of a declared Republican is either a middle-class born-again evangelical who cares most about conservative social issues like the Second Amendment and abortion and hopes for a limited but overtly Christian theocracy, or a corporate baron working behind the scenes to ensure that the rich get richer and the poor don't matter. The impression shouldn't surprise anyone since those are the voices that shout. These voices command large audiences—anywhere from two to five million listeners each day. But is that really so vast? With approximately 55 million registered Republicans, why do we allow so few to speak for so many?

A 2007 Gallup poll reports that only 13 percent of self-declared Republicans describe themselves as "very conservative" (what we usually think of when we think of the far right) while 26 percent describe themselves as "moderate." The poll also indicates that the political positioning of evangelical Christians is also not what the conventional wisdom suggests: "Evangelical Christians, though predominantly conservative, are trending slowly toward the center. The trend is most evident among 18-to 29-year-old white evangelicals...."

Jim Nowlan, in an article written for mywebtimes.com, notes that a recent Pew Center poll found that only 11 percent of registered voters are staunch conservatives. "Political debate in America tends to be framed on cable TV by staunch conservatives such as Glenn Beck and Rush Limbaugh and solid liberals such as Rachel Maddow," he writes. "Yet most of us are neither, according to a major new poll

---

[135] Reviewing the Top 20 list for the Amazon.com category "Political Parties" reveals that nineteen out of the twenty are biased polemics by such authors as Ann Coulter, Glenn Beck, Sean Hannity, and David Mamet. The only outlier is a textbook, *The Logic of American Politics*, coming in at number five. My guess is that the book makes the list because the title is funny.

by the Pew Center for the People and Press, which finds Americans in 2011 fall into nine distinct categories of *homo politicus*."

In addition to "staunch conservatives" the poll also identifies an additional group of key conservatives (termed "Main Street Republicans" in the poll).[136] Members of this group define themselves as conservative on most issues. This additional "key conservative" category adds only another fourteen percentage points to the overall conservative tally, raising the total to an anemic 25 percent. Hardly what many would assume based on the media noise levels. But Nowlan offers a warning to the rest of us:

> Staunch conservatives have an intensity, passion, and uncompromising rigidity on social issues, e.g. pro-life, against homosexuality and same-sex marriage. Because the staunch conservatives are so intense and highly-engaged, they dominate GOP presidential primaries, having influence beyond their numbers.

I'm certainly not arguing against a strong conservative voice in the party. Conservatives have always played an important role in our political history and their consistently strong efforts to reign in government growth and spending recall some of the finest aims of the Republican vision. We work hard and believe others should pull their own weight, too. We respect freedom, resent intrusion, and value both privacy and community. We believe America is great and that we're smart enough and strong enough to fix our problems. Democracy, though not without its flaws, remains the best hope for a peaceful world that respects the rights and needs of individual human beings.

---

[136] Other categories include, for example, "Hard-pressed Democrats," "New Coalition Democrats," and "Disaffecteds."

An America without strong conservative voices would be much less than the America we want it to be. But it's the quality of the voices that we should find so disturbing. People like William F. Buckley, Jr., Barry Goldwater, William Rehnquist, and others added much to our national dialogue by forcing us to think rationally about what are, at heart, ideological issues with no pure answers. All, I believe, would deplore what currently passes for conservative dialogue.

Buckley, arguably one of the most articulate men since Aristotle, wrote in a 2004 article from *The National Review* that:

> Conservatives pride themselves on resisting change, which is as it should be. But intelligent deference to tradition and stability can evolve into intellectual sloth and moral fanaticism, as when conservatives simply decline to look up from dogma because the effort to raise their heads and reconsider is too great.

Contrast Buckley's coherence with Ann Coulter's definition of conservatives:

> Conservatives believe man was created in God's image, while liberals believe they are gods. All of the behavioral tics of the liberals proceed from their godless belief that they can murder the unborn because they, the liberals, are themselves gods. They try to forcibly create "equality" through affirmative action and wealth redistribution because they are gods. They flat-out lie, with no higher power to constrain them, because they are gods. They adore pornography and the mechanization of sex because man is just an animal, and they are gods. They revere the U.N. and not the U.S. because they aren't Americans — they are gods.

Buckley, were he alive today, would likely first gape, then laugh, then tear up at witnessing the cancerian decline of intelligent conservative commentary. Judging by the Twitterverse, right-wing talk radio, and the unruly blogosphere, Buckley's fear has come true: today's neo-cons have declined to "look up from their dogma."

It's the CHiRPs again, and aggressively they tweet.

ೞ ೩

Like a marathoner sprinting the final hundred yards, I'm spending as much time as possible on Twitter, doing what I can to push my ideas and to see where and how they might take root. I'm hoping for kudzu but I'll settle for grape ivy.

For the first part of the week my efforts proved impotent; I realize I'm back where I started, hoping that a single forlorn idea might draw someone's attention in much the same way an abandoned kitten hopes that its tiny mews will bring safety and succor.

Pathetic but hopeful, I drag myself up to my office a few times during the day, check my Twitter timeline, and sigh audibly. My wife asks if anything is wrong, and when I tell her that I'm getting frustrated and depressed again, she offers to drive to Hannaford's and get me a Whoopie Pie.

ೞ ೩

Proving the old cliché that each day brings with it new opportunity, my Twitter feed the next morning shows signs of encouragement:

FindTheCntr: Fellow moderate Republicans: have you noticed that "Moderate" is not in the Republican terminology? We're referred to as Social Conservatives.

It feels like the tweet is just for me and I respond immediately:

BeckIsALib: @FindTheCntr I'm now using the term #consiberal: fiscally conservative and socially moderate, the way the party was for 150 years.

FindTheCntr @BeckIsALib: Consiberal (I like it!)

He then retweets my definition to hundreds of his followers, and the conversation continues:

MidWestMod: I prefer #modcon myself... 'liberal' carries too much baggage.

MidWestMod: @BeckIsALib @FindTheCntr I'd love a term that contains neither conservative or liberal. Both of those terms signal narrow views (cont)

MidWestMod: @BeckIsALib @FindTheCntr (cont) and not an open mind. As a moderate I'd like a term that isn't a hybrid because I'm not just a combination of the two.

FindTheCntr: @ MidWestMod @BeckIsALib The word is "independent."

I disagreed: from my point of view "independent" didn't capture the flavor I'm looking for. It's an "other" term rather than a definition and it doesn't send the signal I want to send: that there is a specific place in the political spectrum for the fiscally conservative and socially moderate Republican. "Modcon" doesn't work either; MidWestMod agreed with me, especially after I told her I'd found out that the word had already been co-opted by those who enjoy some pretty serious body modifications.[137]

> MidWestMod: @BeckIsALib @FindTheCntr Independent is too broad in scope. There are independents across the spectrum from far left to far right.

So *consiberal* it is. The term may not be perfect but now, two days shy of my self-imposed deadline, it's starting to draw a bit of attention. Several other tweeps have expressed curiosity and, perhaps more importantly, I'm noting increased commentary from center-right Republicans much like myself. We're out there after all, just as I suspected.

ೞ ಜ

I've been asking myself a puzzling question for a while now. If I truly believe that Glenn Beck isn't that important, and yet still believe we've seen a sea change in political dialogue, just what is it that's really going on?

The answer came from, of all people, Ron Paul just after the New Hampshire debate, when he remarked on the candidates' mutual civility. When I heard his comment, it all came together for me: civility is now something to comment on instead of just simply being the way we behave. No one truly expected civility during the debate.

---

[137] And when I say "pretty serious," I mean really serious. I downloaded a poorly identified .pdf version of a coffee table book on the subject, then quickly realized that it's only a coffee table book if said coffee table is down in your basement next to the kinds of devices Torquemada used to extract confessions from adjudged heretics.

Perhaps no one truly wanted it—I myself had hoped for a bit of snark—and so civility's presence was actually remarkable.

So Ron Paul remarked on it. I find myself thinking back to the evolution of snark, insult, and defamation, and the way our public figures have embraced these behaviors as a way to get attention, as a way to avoid real conversation and as a way to speak not to our minds (or even our hearts) but to someplace different, someplace darker, where we house our fear and anger and pain. As long as we let them do this to us then we get the leaders we deserve, the lies we deserve and the conversations we deserve.

೮೩ ೮೦

June 15, the Ides of June, arrives. Quite a bit has happened on this day in history. In 1215 King John signed the Magna Carta and in 1664 England claimed New Jersey for the Duke of York, formally establishing the region as a British colony. In 1844 Goodyear patented vulcanized rubber. In 1984 Alan Thicke's *Thicke of the Night* mercifully ended its late-night television run.

In 2011 @BeckIsALib prepares for his closing tweet, the last as an anonymous persona. I end the run having launched over 2,500 tweets, enticing some 600 people to follow me, and conversing with hundreds more. Here and there a few people now entertain the notion that Glenn Beck isn't quite what he seems; here and there the term consiberal, fostered by self-discovery, can be found snaking its way through the Twittermind.

The last tweet in this experiment must be perfect, but I know it won't be. Summing up three months of experience in only 140 characters can't—perhaps shouldn't—be done. Still, I've been playing with drafts for a few days now hoping to alight on the ideal phrasing: part illumination, part revelation, part koan. I'll figure it out; I have until midnight.

In the meantime I've got the rest of today to play with and I'm deciding what to do with my time. Part of me wants to launch a final barrage of tweets, a scheduled flurry of fifteen or twenty consiberal-related thoughts designed to focus the spotlight one last time. The other part of me says, "No. Let's just go out the way we came in—quietly and honestly, without fanfare or expectation."

If I choose the first route then I'm just contributing to the noise, just proving that I'm now one more typical tweep, someone who knows that if you want an audience, you have to scream long and loudly. I do want to, though, if only to see the reaction.

But then that's the point, isn't it? Consiberals are rational people with moderated voices, people who choose to avoid getting sucked down into the mire of political diatribe. I fight the urge.

☙ ❧

It's nearing midnight; the Ides fade and I'm reminded of how I felt just after this thirteenth week began:

I'm tired, frustrated, and cranky, as brain dead as Newt Gingrich on a good day. It's June 10, just five short days away from the Ides, and I can't say that I have much to show for all this effort.

But then again, perhaps I do.

Michael Charney

EPILOGUE:
THE PERFECT TWEET

BeckIsALib: To all with whom I tweet: When I began I thought I was looking for you, but I ended up looking for me. I like what I have found. #Consiberal

Michael Charney

ACKNOWLEDGEMENTS

This book, which started out as a bizarre little idea that I thought might offer some amusement, quickly absorbed the time and attention of quite a few people, and to them I am very gratefully indebted.

Greg Russak, Reine Silverlight-Mallonee, Mary Ann Reilly, Rob Cohen, Fran Sansalone, and Gabe Vanore all read (and re-read) various drafts, and all provided critical and thoughtful feedback, particularly with respect to the overall narrative arc. Without their careful evaluations the book could easily have become a series of disconnected essays (or worse, just a bunch of meandering rants). Rob and Mary Ann also contributed a Jeremy Bentham quote and an epigram, respectively. Rob Traverso and Chris Vetere provided me the younger perspective (and also kept checking in to see what was new on the website). My thanks also go out to Jennifer Newcombe Marine for her sage advice on how to keep the overall effort on track, and to Cindy Sherwood for her excellent editing.

Recently reconnecting with a number of childhood friends (Facebook is a truly wonderful social medium) allowed me to verify and/or flesh out a few of my oldest memories. I'm thankful to

Sharon Russell, Craig Hilton, Hartley Engel, Richard Angelini, Roland Greene, and Jeff Shaw for their help (even though they might not have known they were helping…).

A number of books served as useful references throughout the writing and editing processes. In particular, I found the following exceptionally helpful: Dana Milbank's *Tears of a Clown: Glenn Beck and the Teabagging of America*; Alexander Zaitchik's *Common Nonsense: Glenn Beck and the Triumph of Ignorance*; Jonathan Kay's *Among the Truthers: A Journey Through America's Growing Conspiracist Underground*; Xander Cricket's *Glenn Beck: The Redemptive Story of America's Favorite Political Commentator*; Charles Pierce's *Idiot America: How Stupidity Became a Virtue in the Land of the Free*; Richard Shenkman's *Just How Stupid Are We? Facing the Truth About the American Voter* along with his *Legends, Lies and Cherished Myths of American History*; John Avlon's *Wingnuts: How the Lunatic Fringe is Hijacking America*; Meghan McCain's *Dirty Sexy Politics*; Juan Williams' *Muzzled: The Assault on Honest Debate*; Thomas Frank's *What's the Matter with Kansas? How Conservatives Won the Heart of America*; Michael Shermer's *The Believing Brain: From Ghosts and Gods to Politics and Conspiracies—How We Construct Beliefs and Reinforce Them as Truths*; Carl R. Trueman's *Republocrat: Confessions of a Liberal Conservative*; Senator Barry Goldwater's *Conscience of a Conservative*; Alan Abramowitz's *The Disappearing Center: Engaged Citizens, Polarization, and American Democracy*; and Mickey Edwards' *Reclaiming Conservatism: How a Great American Political Movement Got Lost—and How it Can Find its Way Back*.

Most importantly my wife, Renee, provided not only feedback, but an incredible amount of support as well, giving me plenty of time and space to embark on what I'm sure she thought was just another random obsession.

ABOUT THE AUTHOR

Michael Charney lives in New Hampshire with his wife and two dogs. He enjoys a bit of surrealism now and then, and counts among his friends several people who can quote extensive passages from *Monty Python and the Holy Grail*, *The Hitchhiker's Guide to the Galaxy*, and *Red Dwarf*. A graduate of the University of California, Berkeley, he has managed to become a Republican anyway. He continues to write and converse with others on politics, political dialogue, and political marketing at his website and blog, www.chasingglennbeck.com.

Chasing Glenn Beck

Made in the USA
Lexington, KY
08 June 2012